WILLING AND ABLE

WILLING AND ABLE

A Practical Guide to Powers of Attorney in Ontario

N. Jeanne Best

with Dawn Dudley Oosterhoff

Willing and Able

Second Edition

First Edition: 0-9684488-0-1
October 1998; Reprinted: July 1999

ISBN: 0-9684488-1-X

For more information or to order additional copies, please contact:

Best Associates Paralegal Services
(705) 722-0849

Printed in Canada at Essence Publishing, Belleville, ON, 1-800-238-6376

Table of Contents

Part I   An Introduction to Powers of Attorney

Defining words: attorney, Power of Attorney for Personal Care, Continuing Power of Attorney for Property, advance directive, living will, property, personal care; appointing an attorney

What is the law?
Power of Attorney Act
Substitute Decisions Act
Health Care Consent Act

What is mental capacity?
Presumption of mental capacity
Triggers that signal incapacity
Mental capacity is time and decision dependent

Requirements for giving a Continuing Power of Attorney for Property
Requirements for giving a Power of Attorney for Personal Care
Who decides whether a person is capable of giving a power of attorney?
How do they decide? Witnessing a power of attorney

Part II   Continuing Power of Attorney for Property

Part III   Power of Attorney for Personal Care

Part IV   Some Practical Considerations

Without counsel plans go wrong,
but with many advisors they succeed.
Proverbs 15:22

For Christ is the end of the law,
that every one who has faith may be justified.
Romans 10:4

Preface to the Second Edition

The response to the first edition of *Willing and Able* was excellent and I am pleased now to present a revised and expanded second edition. *Willing and Able* has been reviewed and reflects current legislation but does not provide legal advice. Chapters 3, 6, 10 and 11 have been substantially reorganized to bring greater clarity to the discussions about mental capacity, capacity assessment and decision making on behalf of incapable people. I have added more life stories and further developed the index. Another appendix has been added that provides four charts related to the decision making processes under the *Substitute Decisions Act* and the *Health Care Consent Act.* Information in the charts has been cross referenced with the text of *Willing and Able* as well as applicable legislation.

As I have talked to various groups and my own clients over the past five years it is obvious that understanding and using powers of attorney continues to be difficult for many people. There can be strong feelings and emotions associated with the preparation of powers of attorney. Many approach the task as they would unpleasant medicine: "I don't like talking about these things but I know it's good for me so let's just get it done." I continue to believe that emotions settle and people are well served by the provision of information that is helpful to them in this important area of estate planning.

It is my hope that *Willing and Able* will continue to be a user-friendly reference for anyone who is making or using powers of attorney in Ontario.

Acknowledgments

I sincerely thank Dawn Oosterhoff for her ongoing interest in the field of substitute decision making and her desire to educate others. Dawn not only provided me with the 'kick start' I needed to work on this second edition but has given of her knowledge, time, and writing talents to support my work.

I would also like to thank the many other professionals who took time to discuss, review, and provide useful suggestions for the manuscript of this edition.

Part I

An Introduction to Powers of Attorney

1 Powers of Attorney - Protecting Your Right to Choose

Congratulations! If you've opened this book, you're among a growing number of people who want to understand what a power of attorney in Ontario is all about, how it affects your rights and under what circumstances you should have one. This book will provide you with the information you need in easy to read language and it's laid out so that you can use the book as a ready reference when a particular question or situation develops in your life.

A **Continuing Power of Attorney for Property** is a legal document in which an individual gives someone else the authority to make financial decisions on their behalf while they are mentally capable and/or to act on their behalf if they become mentally incapable of making financial decisions.

A **Power of Attorney for Personal Care** is a legal document in which an individual gives someone else the authority to make personal care decisions on their behalf if they become incapable of making personal care decisions.

In this chapter ...

- **what a power of attorney is**

- **reasons why people avoid making powers of attorney**

- **different decisions, different documents**

   o   **property**

   o   **personal care**

- **appointing an attorney**

What is a power of attorney?

Very simply, a power of attorney is a legal document in which you appoint, or give power to, an attorney to act on your behalf. Attorney simply means representative. In the United States, lawyers are called Attorneys at Law ("attorneys" for short), meaning legal representatives. In Canada, we call lawyers Barristers and Solicitors.

The word attorney in a power of attorney does not mean a lawyer.

Attorney is the name given to the person you have appointed in a

- General Power of Attorney

  to make property decisions for you while you are mentally capable, but in need of assistance for a period of time or for a specified transaction(s).

- Continuing Power of Attorney for Property

  to make property decisions for you while you are still mentally capable, but want assistance making property decisions; and is continuing because it is still effective if you ever become mentally incapable of making decisions about your property.

- Power of Attorney for Personal Care

  to make personal care decisions for you if you ever become incapable of making your own personal care decisions.

Note: The law makes provision for a general or continuing power of attorney. A bank power of attorney is simply the name given to a power of attorney that you make at the bank. It can be general or continuing - check the wording!

When you make someone your attorney it's because you believe that person will make your decisions just the way you would, if you could. So your attorney must be someone whom you trust to follow your wishes.

If powers of attorney are important, why do so few people have them?

Some people are intimidated when they think about a power of attorney. On the one hand, we worry about the role of government in the affairs of private individuals; on the other hand, we fail to take advantage of the opportunity to appoint someone else to act on our behalf. We tend to fear or avoid what we don't understand even though what we don't understand may be helpful. For many people the laws about powers of attorney are a mystery.

The language of our laws is very technical and most of us would consider the reading of legislation to be a little over our heads, not to mention boring. Let's face it, a copy of the *Substitute Decisions Act[1]* is not likely to be found on the average person's night table. Even if you did buy a copy of the *Substitute Decisions Act* and read it, it wouldn't answer all of your questions. There isn't just one Act (law) that will tell you everything you always wanted to know about a power of attorney. In fact, there are at least four Acts that govern our decision making when we're no longer capable of making our own decisions. The interrelated nature of these laws makes it all seem like a bowl of spaghetti; but don't despair. The pages that follow will talk about the laws and their relationship to one another and the information is condensed and organized so that it's easy to digest.

Apart from our discomfort with the law, there are other reasons why people don't have powers of attorney:

- we procrastinate

  Not having a power of attorney isn't likely to keep you awake at night. It gets added to that list of things we intend to do, but never complete.

- we deny our frailty

  We prefer not to think about ill health or accidents or anything else that might cause us to become incapable of making our own decisions. We never think about who would make our decisions if we couldn't.

- we make it a financial decision

  We don't feel the cost warrants the possibility that a power of attorney would ever be needed or used.

Why should I consider making a power of attorney?

Situations where you may not be able to make decisions for yourself might include medical conditions such as a stroke, Alzheimer Disease, or cancer. Or, as the result of an accident, you might be in a coma and unable to make decisions. Our ability to make our own decisions is something that can change gradually or it can change suddenly and without warning. Whatever the reason, we each need to ask ourselves:

- Who would make my decisions for me if I became incapable?

- How would they know what I wanted or how I would decide if I could?

These questions focus our attention in two areas:

- selection of a person to act on my behalf

- communication of my wishes and instructions to that person

> **Even though the language of our laws can be difficult and the answer to a specific question may be hard to find, the laws are good and they accomplish what they set out to do - protect your right to appoint someone else to act on your behalf.**

In Ontario, the *Substitute Decisions Act* gives you the right to choose in advance who would act on your behalf if you were to become incapable of making property or personal care decisions. If you do not have a power of attorney and become incapable of making a property or personal care decision, then the law says who will make decisions for you. Do you know:

- who the law would designate to act on your behalf if you became mentally incapable?

- who the law would designate as an alternate decision maker if that first person was unable to act on your behalf?

> **One of the most important reasons for making a power of attorney is to ensure that the person you choose is given the authority to act on your behalf when you want them to.**

Different decisions, different documents

The types of decisions that an attorney can make fall into two categories:

- property

- personal care

Property decisions, like banking, paying bills, renewing term investments, and so on, tend to be more objective than personal care decisions, which affect your body, your health and your personal well being. Personal care decisions tend to be intimate decisions.

Property

Use of the word property as it relates to powers of attorney means more than land or real estate. When the law talks about property management and powers of attorney for property, property includes any type of financial decision that a person would make in the course of managing their income, spending, assets and debts. This could include paying bills, filing tax returns, buying or selling real estate, and making investments or loans. In Ontario, there are two different powers of attorney for property:

- General Power of Attorney

This power of attorney is used if a mentally capable person wants to appoint someone to act on their behalf. It could be used for a specific period of time or for a specific transaction. It ends if the person who gives it revokes it or becomes mentally incapable.

- Continuing Power of Attorney for Property

This power of attorney is used if a mentally capable person wants to appoint someone to act on their behalf while they are mentally capable and/or to act on their behalf in the event of mental incapacity.

Note: A General Power of Attorney is limited in its scope and use. It is mentioned here for the information of the reader, but the focus of this book is Continuing Powers of Attorney for Property and Powers of Attorney for Personal Care.

Personal care

Personal care as defined in the law includes health care, shelter, nutrition, clothing, hygiene and safety. The laws that govern personal care decision making for incapable people are provincial laws and each province has adopted their own words and terminology. What we find from one province to another are similar words used in different ways and sometimes different words used in similar ways. Confusing? You bet it is! It may be interesting to know what's happening in other provinces but if it leads to uncertainty about what you can or cannot do in your own province (Ontario), it really is more of a hindrance than a help.

In Ontario, confusion surrounds the use of documents that are called Living Wills or Advance Health Care Directives. Some people use these to write instructions about treatment or end of life care. It's confusing because instructions about personal care can also be written in a Power of Attorney for Personal Care. Uncertainty about how these documents differ and how they can be used is one of the reasons that many people have not exercised their right to appoint an attorney for personal care. It's important for residents of Ontario to understand the words and terminology that are used in Ontario.

Living Wills and Advance Health Care Directives: Where did they come from? Where do they fit in?

The use of Advance Health Care Directives and Living Wills began as a response to changes that were happening in our society. In the late 70's and early 80's there was an increasing public awareness of the rights of individuals to make their own decisions and of the processes that enabled them to exercise those rights. Politically, there was much debate and media coverage surrounding the *Canadian Charter of Rights and Freedoms*[2] and its inclusion in the Canadian constitution. Medically, the *Canadian Patient's Book of Rights*, written by Lorne Rozovsky in 1980,[3] marked the beginning of an era in which physicians were no longer seen as having authority with respect to treatment decisions. People became more aware that they had the right to be informed about their diagnosis and treatment options. This right was further emphasized by a physician's obligation (upheld in common law) to obtain a patient's informed consent to whatever treatment the physician might propose.

This desire for greater autonomy was then coupled with a developing medical technology that was changing the nature of health care decisions and decision making. Rapid advances in medical technology and an increased ability to save and extend life made people realize that life sustaining equipment could keep them living and breathing after an accident or illness that might have been fatal a few years ago. Given the choice, would a person want to be kept alive by artificial means?

Cardiopulmonary resuscitation (CPR), transfusions and intravenous fluids all became routine practice in hospital emergency rooms. Fearing medical heroics in an emergency situation, people began to write down what their wishes would be if they were ever in a situation where they were incapable of making a treatment decision and had to depend on others to make decisions for them.

John Carson had been living with the pain of cancer for two years. He had accepted that he was dying and was now moving in and out of coma. When he developed pneumonia, his doctor suggested antibiotic treatment. Because John's wife knew of John's request to die peacefully without further treatment, his wife refused to consent to the antibiotic treatment.

Mona Harper was a 96 year old woman, living at the Willow Valley Nursing Home. She had lived a long, full life and had no desire to prolong her life by artificial means in the event of a medical emergency. The administrator of the Home had discussed this with Mona when she was admitted. Mona had recorded her wishes in a Living Will and had communicated these wishes to her family and to nursing home staff. Mona was taken to the emergency department one night suffering from a heart attack. After arriving at the hospital, Mona had a cardiac arrest. Because she had prepared an advance directive and had communicated her wishes, she was allowed to die peacefully without resuscitation.

Before the *Substitute Decisions Act,* a Living Will or Advance Health Care Directive had no legal authority. In other words, there was no law that told people they had to respect and follow what had been written in an Advance Health Care Directive or Living Will. Health care professionals and family only had a moral obligation to abide by the wishes that a person had expressed in an advance directive. The *Substitute Decisions Act* and the *Health Care Consent Act* changed this. Now there is an obligation for an attorney or substitute decision maker to follow any wishes or instructions that an incapable person gave while they were capable (unless it is impossible to follow those wishes or instructions).

The *Substitute Decisions Act* introduced the Power of Attorney for Personal Care in which a person could appoint an attorney to act on his or her behalf and could also give instructions to the attorney. Whether the instructions are verbal, written in a separate document (Advance Health Care Directive, Living Will), or included in a Power of Attorney for Personal Care, the legal obligation to follow the instructions is the same.

Advance Directive is a general term that simply means the expression of wishes (written or verbal) made by a person while they were capable of understanding the statement and the consequences associated with making or not making a decision.

Living Will or Advance Health Care Directive are the different names given to the documents in which people write down their wishes and instructions related to personal care.

Appointing an attorney

It is a good idea to meet and talk with a lawyer or trained professional when you decide to make a power of attorney. A knowledgeable professional can discuss your needs with you and answer your questions. Because the nature of a property decision and the nature of a personal care decision are so different, you should never assume that the person you select as your attorney for property should also be your attorney for personal care.

Mary Watson is a 65 year old widow with three sons. Mary's husband died and left her with considerable assets. As part of her estate planning, Mary has identified the need for powers of attorney. Her oldest son, John, is an accountant who lives about an hour away and visits her once a month. Her second son, Bob, manages a paint store. He lives about half an hour away and visits Mary about once a month. Mary feels a close kinship with her youngest son, Tony, a computer programmer who is still living at home. After meeting and talking with her lawyer, Mary decided to appoint her sons John and Bob to be her attorneys for property and to appoint Tony to be her attorney for personal care.

There may be reasons for you to appoint an attorney for property, but not appoint an attorney for personal care. You may want to appoint multiple attorneys. Whatever your situation, each type of power of attorney needs to be discussed separately in relation to you as a person, to the people that are a part of your life, and to your individual circumstances in life.

As we end this chapter, **Important Things to Remember are:**

- **A General Power of Attorney lets you appoint an attorney to make property decisions for you while you are mentally capable. This type of power ends if the person who gives it becomes mentally incapable.**

- **A Continuing Power of Attorney for Property lets you decide who will make financial and property decisions for you while you are capable and/or if you become mentally incapable.**

- **A Power of Attorney for Personal Care lets you decide who will make personal care decisions for you if you become mentally incapable.**

- **If you choose not to appoint an attorney in a power of attorney, the law says who will make your decisions if you are not able.**

- **The person you choose as your attorney must follow any wishes or instructions that you have given, unless it is impossible for your attorney to do so.**

- **Wishes or instructions regarding personal care may be written in a Power of Attorney for Personal Care or written in another document (Living Will, Advance Directive, etc.) or they may be verbal instructions that you expressed to those who care and make decisions for you.**

2 Powers of Attorney and the Law

In the Province of Ontario, there are several laws that protect your right to appoint someone else to act on your behalf. These laws make it possible for you to appoint an attorney in a power of attorney.

In this chapter …

- **a general description of what the law is**

- **an overview of the applicable laws**

    o   *Powers of Attorney Act*

    o   *Substitute Decisions Act*

    o   *Health Care Consent Act*

What do we mean when we use the word law?

In Canada, the basis of the legal system is called the English Common Law (except in Quebec, where the law is based on a Civil Code system). The English Common Law is the collection of rules established by judges when they hear cases. In addition to the Common Law, law is found in the Acts and Statutes of parliament and provincial legislatures, and in the by-laws of municipalities. Under the authority of Statutes, other Boards and Commissions may be given the power to make regulations, rules and policies. Along with the Common Law, all of these things constitute the law.

The law reflects the values of society and it works to establish principles that will guard and protect what is important and accepted by society as a whole. The law is constantly needing to change because the way people relate to one another in a society is constantly changing. Often it seems the law is slow to change but this is because it always follows the evolution of society's values and relationships that are also slow to change.

The laws discussed in this book protect certain rights. A right is something that you are entitled to and at the same time, is something that someone else has a duty to give you. Without the law, there is no legal duty and without a legal duty, there can be no right because there is nothing that a court of law can enforce.[4]

Consider again the questions that were asked before:

- Who would make my decisions for me if I became incapable?

- How would they know what I wanted or how I would decide if I could?

The *Powers of Attorney Act*[5] and the *Substitute Decisions Act* are the two laws that give you the right to appoint an attorney in a power of attorney. Once acting on your behalf, your attorney has a legal duty to you, a duty to make decisions in your best interest and according to your instructions.

Ontario laws that protect your decision making rights

Powers of Attorney Act

In Ontario, prior to 1995, the *Powers of Attorney Act* was the law that enabled a person to appoint an attorney in a General Power of Attorney. Most of the *Powers of Attorney Act* was repealed (withdrawn) when the new laws about substitute decision making (*Substitute Decisions Act, Health Care Consent Act*[6]) were introduced. However, the *Powers of Attorney Act* still gives you the right to appoint an attorney in a General Power of Attorney to make property decisions on your behalf. A General Power of Attorney, therefore, continues to be a legally recognized document.

A person who gives a Power of Attorney is called a grantor.

Historically, one of the problems with a General Power of Attorney was that it was no longer effective when the person who gave it (the grantor) became mentally incapable. In 1979, a provision was added to this law so that people could make their General Power of Attorney a "continuing" power of attorney, that is, the authority of the attorney would continue after any subsequent mental incapacity of the grantor. This provision was repealed in 1995 and in its place the *Substitute Decisions Act* introduced what is called a Continuing Power of Attorney for Property.

You can appoint an attorney in a General Power of Attorney to make property decisions on your behalf while you are mentally capable. However, if a person wants to appoint an attorney in anticipation of future mental incapacity, whether it be from accident, injury, or ill health, they should make a Continuing Power of Attorney for Property under the authority and rules of the *Substitute Decisions Act*.

A power of attorney is called continuing because it can be used after the grantor is no longer mentally capable. The word durable is also used by some people and means the same as continuing.

With the introduction of a Continuing Power of Attorney for Property, the use of a General Power of Attorney has become more limited and relates to specific periods of time or events. For example, if a person is out of the country and needs someone to manage their financial affairs temporarily, they can appoint an attorney under a General Power of Attorney; or, if a person is in hospital recovering from surgery and they need someone to complete a real estate transaction on their behalf, they can appoint an attorney to act on their behalf under a General Power of Attorney.

Use of a General Power of Attorney usually involves financial transactions at the bank and you will need to specify the nature of the authority that you are giving to your attorney. The bank will ask you to:

- visit the bank with your attorney

- complete a General Power of Attorney form that the bank provides

- sign the form, which is then witnessed by a bank employee(s)

- have your attorney sign a bank card so that their signature is on file

In summary, a General Power of Attorney (for property) is used when you need someone to act on your behalf for a specific period of time or for a specific financial transaction. A Continuing Power of Attorney for Property lets you appoint an attorney to act on your behalf while you are mentally capable and/or if you become mentally incapable.

Substitute Decisions Act

The *Substitute Decisions Act* is the law that governs the appointment of an attorney for property in a Continuing Power of Attorney for Property and the appointment of an attorney for personal care in a Power of Attorney for Personal Care. The new Act was introduced by one government and then once enacted, was substantially revised by another government the following year. At the same time there were changes to other related laws.

In March 1995, three new laws came into effect:

- the *Advocacy Act*[7]

- the *Consent to Treatment Act*[8]

- the *Substitute Decisions Act*

These new laws recognized that:

- there were different types of decisions

- a person's capacity to make a decision might be adequate in one area or at one time, but not in another area or at another time

In June 1995, a new government made the review of these three laws a priority on their agenda. Within one year (in March 1996):

- the *Advocacy Act* was repealed

- the Substitute Decisions Act was revised

- the *Consent to Treatment Act* was replaced by the *Health Care Consent Act*

The purpose of these changes was:

- to simplify some of the complex procedures in the new laws

- to reinforce the positive role of families and service providers

- to bring better balance between the individual's right to control their own life and the responsibility of society to protect incapable, vulnerable individuals.

The first part of the *Substitute Decisions Act* provides us with information about making and using a Continuing Power of Attorney for Property. It discusses capacity to give a Continuing Power of Attorney for Property, the appointment of an attorney, revocation or termination of the power of attorney and duties of an attorney or guardian of property. The procedures under which the Public Guardian and Trustee would become a person's statutory guardian of property are outlined, as are procedures for court-appointed guardianship of property.

The second part of the *Substitute Decisions Act* provides us with information about making and using a Power of Attorney for Personal Care. It discusses capacity to give a power of attorney for personal care, when the power of attorney is effective, the appointment of an attorney, revocation or termination of the power of attorney and duties of an attorney or guardian of the person. Application procedures for court- appointed guardians of the person are also given.

Health Care Consent Act

The *Health Care Consent Act* provides the rules for obtaining consent for treatment and substitute decision making in relation to certain health care decisions. It provides a definition of mental capacity and talks about who should assess mental capacity in relation to decisions about treatment, admission to a Long Term Care facility and personal assistance services in a Long Term Care facility. The *Health Care Consent Act* is also the law that establishes the Consent and Capacity Board.

Personal Care includes health care, nutrition, shelter, clothing, hygiene, and safety (*Substitute Decisions Act* (section 45)).

The three types of health care decisions covered by this law are:

- treatment
- admission to a Long Term Care facility
- personal assistance services in a Long Term Care facility

The *Health Care Consent Act* makes it a legal duty for anyone proposing treatment or care for a person to first obtain the consent of the person for whom the treatment or care is proposed or, if the person is incapable, from their substitute decision maker.

Treatment

Treatment means anything that is done for a therapeutic, preventive, palliative, diagnostic, cosmetic or other health related purpose, including a course of treatment or plan of treatment. Treatment does not include assessment of capacity, general assessment of a person's condition, taking of a health history, communication of a diagnosis, admission to a hospital, personal assistance services, or treatment that under the circumstances poses little or no risk. Any health practitioner who is proposing a treatment for someone else must obtain the consent of the person or the person's substitute decision maker if the person is not mentally capable for this purpose.

Admission to Long Term Care facilities

This applies to the admission of people to beds in government licensed and funded Long Term Care facilities. Long Term Care facilities may also be called Nursing Homes or Homes for the Aged. This section of the *Health Care Consent Act* does not apply to the admission of people to privately owned and operated retirement homes. (Note: Retirement homes are not Long Term Care facilities. Retirement homes are tenancies and are referred to as "Care Homes" under the *Tenant Protection Act*[9].)

The process for admitting a person to a Long Term Care facility is the responsibility of the local Community Care Access Centre (CCAC). Admission to a Long Term Care facility must be authorized by staff of the CCAC, but admission can only be authorized if the person or, if the person is incapable, their substitute first gives consent to the admission. There is provision for admission without consent in a crisis situation, but then consent must be obtained as soon as possible after the admission.

Personal assistance services in a Long Term Care facility

Personal assistance services are services that provide help with or supervision of hygiene, washing, dressing, grooming, eating, drinking, elimination, ambulation, positioning, or any other routine activity of living. Under the *Health Care Consent Act*, if a person is unable to make decisions about these services, a substitute decision maker may make decisions on the person's behalf. Personal assistance services refer to those services provided in the Long Term Care facilities to which Part III (Admission to Care Facilities) of the Act applies. The *Health Care Consent Act* does not apply to personal assistance services that might be provided in a person's home or in privately owned and operated care homes (retirement homes).

Consent and Capacity Board

The *Health Care Consent Act* is the law that establishes the Consent and Capacity Board; a tribunal created by the provincial government for the purpose of hearing matters under the *Health Care Consent Act,* the *Mental Health Act*, the *Substitute Decisions Act*, and the *Long Term Care Act*. It operates independently of health care institutions, government agencies, doctors and other health professionals. It is not a court and only has powers that the law gives to it. (See Chapter 14 for further information.)

As we end this chapter, **Important Things to Remember are:**

- The *Powers of Attorney Act* is the law that gives you the right to appoint an attorney for property under a General Power of Attorney (for property).

- The *Substitute Decisions Act* is the law that gives you the right to appoint

    o an attorney for property under a Continuing Power of Attorney for Property

    o an attorney for personal care under a Power of Attorney for Personal Care.

- The *Health Care Consent Act* deals with three types of health care decisions: treatment, admission to a Long Term Care facility, and personal assistance services in a Long Term Care facility.

- With regard to these three types of decisions, the *Health Care Consent Act* says that a person has the right to decide whether to give or refuse consent to anything being proposed for them if they are mentally capable for that purpose.

- The *Health Care Consent Act* is the law that establishes the Consent and Capacity Board.

3 Mental Capacity
A Framework for Decision Making

Our society believes that a person who is mentally capable and able to understand their situation has the right to make their own decisions.

In this chapter ...

- **mental capacity defined**

- **presumption of mental capacity**

    o **triggers that signal incapacity**

    o **what mental capacity is not based on**

- **mental capacity is time and decision dependent**

Mental capacity as it relates to decision making and powers of attorney is an important concept. The purpose of this chapter is to introduce the concept of mental capacity for decision making. Specific information about the assessment of mental capacity and its application to property and personal care decisions is discussed later in the book.

Mental capacity defined

In the past, a person was considered to be either mentally competent or incompetent. Competence was a concept that lacked definition. The process of assessing competence often led to an all or nothing judgment of a person's ability to make any decisions pertaining to him or herself. But competence is more than this. It is a complex part of our person and our ability for a given task at a given time. In their book, *When the Mind Fails*, Michael Silberfeld and Arthur Fish provide an insightful description of what competency is:

> When talking about competency and incompetency we are dealing with matters that lie close to the core of our humanity. The word competent literally means 'having sufficient ability to perform a specific task,' and it is related to a number of other terms, like independence, self-esteem, and happiness, that are commonly used to describe the qualities of a life that is worth living. Competency is a person's ability to make, and act on, his or her own decisions. The ability to decide what to do, and then to do it, is closely connected with how people feel and think about themselves and how others think and feel about them: a person's competency, in large measure, is what he or she is.[10]

The words competent and incompetent are used less frequently now and have, for the most part, been replaced by use of the words capable and incapable. The *Mental Health Act* continues to use the words competence and incompetence when describing a person's ability to make decisions but both the *Substitute Decisions Act* and *the Health Care Consent Act* use the words capable and incapable.

Our society believes that a person who is mentally capable and able to understand their situation has the right to make their own decisions. A person has the right to receive whatever information is relevant to a decision and to know what his or her choices are in a given situation.

In Ontario, mental capacity is a legal definition; it is not a medical condition or mental health status.

Section 6 of the *Substitute Decisions Act* states that a person is capable of managing property if the person is able to understand information that is relevant to making a decision in the management of his or her property, and is able to appreciate the reasonably foreseeable consequences of a decision or lack of decision.

Section 4 of the *Health Care Consent Act* states that a person is capable with respect to a treatment, an admission to a care facility or a personal assistance service if the person is able to understand the information that is relevant to making a decision about the treatment, admission, or personal assistance service, as the case may be, and able to appreciate the reasonably foreseeable consequences of a decision or lack of decision.

Sally Smith found a drawer of unpaid bills when she came to visit her father, who had suffered a mild stroke six months earlier. When asked about them, her father simply replied, "Oh yeah, I figure they'll call me if there's a problem." Joe Smith understood that he had not paid his bills, but his ability to appreciate the consequences was impaired. He failed to recognize the financial implication (having to pay to have service reconnected) or the possible personal implication (no heat or light).

There are some people with whom you can carry on what seems to be a normal conversation. They pass the first test of understanding what is being said to them. The concept makes sense and they grasp the information. On further questioning, however, it is evident that they fail to appreciate how certain choices will affect them. There is a lack of reasoning and judgment skill, and an inability to apply the information to their own life and situation. For example, a non-recovered alcoholic may understand that drinking too much is a problem and then deny that he has a problem. He understands the concept of drinking too much but fails to appreciate the consequences that excessive drinking are having in his own life.

In decision making, the person must understand and appreciate information about the decision and must also understand and appreciate the consequences of making or not making the decision. A person demonstrates mental capacity to make a decision when both aspects of the definition are present and working together. A teenage girl may understand and appreciate information about a diagnosis of anorexia and about the treatment that is offered to her. At the same time, her refusal of tube feeding may demonstrate an inability to understand and appreciate that the consequence of her decision could result in death.

Presumption of mental capacity

> **A person is always presumed to be mentally capable, unless there is reason to believe that they are not.**

The *Substitute Decisions Act* and the *Health Care Consent Act* tell us that a person is presumed to be capable, unless there is reason to believe that they are not. The assessment of mental capacity should always be approached from that perspective. People can make good decisions and they can make bad decisions. A bad decision is not usually a signal of incapacity. Sometimes there are other reasons for suspecting that someone is incapable and these are called triggers. Triggers that might prompt further investigation of a person's mental capacity include:

- unusual behaviour

- disorientation to time, person or place

- lack of reasonable judgment or memory

- anxiety, depression

- repetitive speech or aggression

Questioning a person's capacity is very serious and needs to be approached with much care and caution. There is always the risk that a capable person will be incorrectly assessed or that the degree of a person's incapacity will be exaggerated. It is helpful to know that the determination of a person's mental capacity is **not** based on:

- their medical diagnosis

  Just because someone has a diagnosis of Alzheimer Disease or Multiple Sclerosis doesn't mean they have lost their ability to make a particular decision at a particular point in time.

- their age

  There is no minimum age of consent in Ontario. A person is never incapable because of their age.

- their agreement or disagreement with a proposed treatment or other act

  Sometimes professionals feel that they know what's best for another person. Just because a person doesn't agree with the recommendation of a professional doesn't mean the person is incapable.

- whether they have a disability

  Just because someone has a speech, hearing, or physical impairment doesn't mean that they are mentally incapable.

Mental capacity is time and decision dependent

Mental capacity to make a decision has to do with a person's ability to receive and process information at a particular point in time. There is a more realistic belief now that one's ability (mental capacity) to make a decision should be in relation to an individual decision or group of decisions. Mental incapacity occurs when there is a block in one's ability to do this. Things that might create a block could include:

- a mental disorder

  The laws for substitute decision making apply to people who suffer from mental disorders, but the concept of mental incapacity is different than that of mental disorder. Capacity is a legal definition. Mental disorder is a health condition or diagnosis.

- lack of consciousness

Blocks may be partial or intermittent. A person may be mentally capable of making some decisions, but not others. This is referred to as partial capacity. A person may be mentally capable at certain points in time, but not at other times. This is referred to as intermittent capacity.

Partial capacity

- A person with dementia may enjoy smoking, but forget that they just lit a cigarette or forget to use an ashtray. If their care giver keeps the cigarettes and monitors their use, the person can smoke safely. Without supervision the person might set their clothes on fire or cause harm to others.

Intermittent capacity

- A person who suffers from a mental disorder like schizophrenia or manic-depression may pay their rent and other bills on time for many months at a time, but if they become delusional or immobile because of their illness, they may need temporary assistance to make sure the bills are paid.

- A person with Alzheimer disease may be able to make a decision in the morning about what they want to wear that day but become confused and disoriented later in the day and need help and reminding not to go outside in the cold without a coat. Intermittent capacity can occur even within the space of a few hours.

Our laws encourage the involvement of a person in decision making to the extent that he or she is capable. For family and care givers there is always a fine balance between society's obligation to protect its vulnerable members and the right of a person to make the decisions that they have capacity to make.

> **Mental capacity cannot be determined by asking questions that only require yes or no answers. Questioning must open the way for the person to express their understanding, feelings, and opinion about a particular situation and the decision that is required.**

Judgment about a person's mental capacity can only be made by communicating with the person about the issue at hand and being satisfied that:

- they understand and appreciate what's being said to them

- they understand and appreciate the reasonable, foreseeable consequences of their decision or lack of decision

The intent here is not to simplify the complex nature of capacity assessment or to underestimate the skill that is required to evaluate another person's understanding and appreciation. The process by which a person's capacity is determined is valuative and often difficult. It can create the ethical dilemmas with which we as a society struggle.

As we end this chapter, **Important Things to Remember are:**

- **In Ontario, capacity is a legal definition.**

- **Mental capacity, as defined in the *Substitute Decisions Act* and the *Health Care Consent Act,* includes:**

   o   **the ability to understand information relevant to making a decision**

   o   **the ability to appreciate the reasonable, foreseeable consequences of making or not making a decision.**

- **A person is presumed to be mentally capable unless there is evidence to believe otherwise.**

- **A person may be capable of some decisions but not of others (partial capacity).**

- **A person may be capable of decisions at certain points in time but not at other times (intermittent capacity).**

4   Capacity to Give a Power of Attorney

Before applying the concept of mental capacity to specific property and personal care decisions, it is important to recognize that a person must be mentally capable of giving a power of attorney.

In this chapter …

- **requirements for giving a Continuing Power of Attorney for Property**

- **requirements for giving a Power of Attorney for Personal Care**

- **who decides whether a person is capable of giving a power of attorney**

- **witnessing a power of attorney**

The need for a power of attorney arises when a person becomes incapable of managing either their property or personal care. If the need is identified and the person has not yet appointed an attorney then the question should always be asked, "Is the person capable of appointing an attorney for property in a Continuing Power of Attorney for Property and/or an attorney for personal care in a Power of Attorney for Personal Care?" A person may have lost their mental capacity with respect to managing their property or personal care, but they may still be able to appoint an attorney to make decisions on their behalf. (See Appendix A: Figure 1)

> **A person who gives a power of attorney is called a grantor or donor.**
> **A person who becomes the attorney is called the grantee or donee.**

Capacity to give Continuing Power of Attorney for Property

The requirements that measure a person's capacity to give a Continuing Power of Attorney for Property are outlined in the *Substitute Decisions Act* (section 8) and are as follows. The person must:

- know what kind of property they have and its approximate value

- be aware of obligations owed to dependents

- know that the attorney will be able to do anything on their behalf that they could do if capable, except make a will (subject to conditions and/or restrictions set out in the power of attorney)

- know that the attorney must give an account for the way they manage the property

- know that the continuing power of attorney can be revoked as long as they are mentally capable

- appreciate that the value of their property may decline unless the attorney manages the property prudently

- appreciate the possibility that the attorney could misuse the authority given to them

Capacity to give a Power of Attorney for Personal Care

The requirements that measure a person's ability to give a Continuing Power of Attorney for Property are much more detailed and specific than those which measure ability to give a Power of Attorney for Personal Care. The threshold of capacity to appoint an attorney for personal care is much lower than it is for property. These requirements are found in the *Substitute Decisions Act* (section 47 (1)) and are as follows.

- a person must have the ability to understand whether the proposed attorney has a genuine concern for the person's welfare

- the person must appreciate that the person may need to have the proposed attorney make decisions on the person's behalf

A person may have lost their mental capacity with respect to managing their personal care or understanding the consequences of a personal care decision, but they may still be able to appoint an attorney for personal care. As long as the person knows that the proposed attorney has a concern for their welfare and may have to make decisions for them, they are mentally capable of giving a Power of Attorney for Personal Care.

Capacity to give instructions in a Power of Attorney for Personal Care

Although the threshold of mental capacity to give a Power of Attorney for Personal Care is low, the *Substitute Decisions Act* provides the grantor with some protection against the inclusion of instructions that they may not understand or appreciate. The Act stipulates that the grantor must be mentally capable with respect to any instructions that are given in the document (*Substitute Decisions Act* (section 47 (4)). In other words, the grantor must understand the nature of the instruction and the consequences of including the instruction. If, for example, a person is considering end of life care and the use of life supports, the magnitude of instructions related to these decisions is much greater than simply naming an attorney. Therefore, a person may be capable of giving a Power of Attorney for Personal Care, but not capable of including instructions in it.

Albert Bell is a 54 year old man with Parkinson's Disease who suffers from moderate dementia. Albert appointed his wife Anna as his attorney for property in 1991 in a General Power of Attorney. The power of attorney makes provision for it to be a "continuing" power of attorney and it continues to meet the needs of the Bells. Anna feels that she should also have a Power of Attorney for Personal Care and takes Albert to see the lawyer to have one prepared. Albert has difficulty talking and answering questions. It is evident that he looks to Anna to answer for him and stays close to her side. Despite his behaviour and limited response to questioning, the lawyer feels Albert is able to give a Power of Attorney for Personal Care to his wife. Because of his dementia, however, Albert is not mentally capable of discussing and making decisions about instructions such as end of life treatment or care, so the document is written with no conditions, restrictions or instructions.

Who decides whether a person is capable of giving a power of attorney?

The *Substitute Decisions Act* does not directly answer this question. The fact that it gives us criteria by which to evaluate whether a person is capable of giving a power of attorney indicates that mental capacity to give a power of attorney could be challenged if the criteria were not met. The grantor's mental capacity to give a power of attorney should be evaluated during the interview, prior to the preparation of the document(s). If the grantor doesn't appear to meet the criteria and capacity to give the power of attorney is in question, it is wise to seek professional help and advice from someone trained to assess capacity.

Anyone assisting someone else in the preparation of a power of attorney has a duty to ensure that the person is capable of giving the power of attorney.

With respect to the evaluation of mental capacity to give a Continuing Power of Attorney for Property, it is important that the grantor be given the opportunity to express him or herself and not simply answer 'yes' or 'no' to simple questions. There must be a discussion with the grantor to ensure that the grantor understands what property they have and what it's worth. The grantor's intentions with respect to their finances must be understood.

Examples of poor questions that prompt 'yes' or 'no' answers are:

- Do you know what property you have?

- Do you know what your property is worth?

- Do you know that you can revoke this power of attorney?

Examples of good questions which make it clear that the person is capable (or not capable) of giving the power of attorney are:

- What property do you own?

- How much is your property worth?

- What can you do if you don't think your attorney is acting in your best interest?

The same principle applies in the preparation of a Power of Attorney for Personal Care. Again, it is important that the grantor express his or her feelings and wishes and not simply answer 'yes' or 'no' to simple questions. Examples of poor questions are:

- Do you think the person you have chosen to be your attorney has a genuine concern for your welfare?

- Do you appreciate that your attorney may have to make decisions for you?

Examples of good questions which help to clarify whether the person is capable (or not capable) of giving a Power of Attorney for Personal Care are:

- How do you know that the person you have chosen as your attorney has a genuine concern for your welfare?

- What kind of relationship have you had with this person?

- How have they helped you in the past?

- What made you choose them?

- What kinds of decisions would you want them to make for you if you were not able to make your own decisions?

If the grantor wants to include instructions about medical care and treatment they might want to discuss this with their doctor and their religious advisor. Any specific instructions should also be discussed with the proposed attorney to ensure that the attorney is prepared to follow such instructions.

Witnessing a power of attorney

After the power of attorney is prepared, it must be signed and witnessed by two people in the presence of the grantor and each other. Witnesses have no legal duty to determine whether someone is capable or incapable. A witness is only verifying that the person signing the power of attorney is the grantor. Further information about the witnessing of powers of attorney can be found in Chapter 5 and Chapter 9.

As we end this chapter, **Important Things to Remember are:**

- **A person must be mentally capable of giving a power of attorney.**

- **The criteria that indicate whether a person is mentally capable of giving a power of attorney are found in the *Substitute Decisions Act.***

- **A person must be mentally capable with respect to any instructions about personal care that are included in a Power of Attorney for Personal Care.**

- **Anyone who assists a person in the preparation of a power of attorney has a duty to ensure that the person is capable of giving the power of attorney.**

Part II

Continuing Power of Attorney for Property

5 Rules and Requirements related to a Continuing Power of Attorney for Property

A Continuing Power of Attorney for Property is a legal document in which an individual gives someone else the authority to make financial decisions on their behalf while they are capable and/or to act on their behalf in the event of mental incapacity. The rules and requirements discussed in this chapter come from the *Substitute Decisions Act*.

In this chapter …

- **who can give a Continuing Power of Attorney for Property**

- **who can be an attorney for property**

- **what decisions can be made by an attorney for property**

- **the duties of an attorney for property**

- **the requirements for witnessing a Continuing Power of Attorney for Property**

- **when a Continuing Power of Attorney for Property becomes effective**

- **cancelling, terminating, or revoking a Continuing Power of Attorney for Property**

What is a Continuing Power of Attorney for Property?

A Continuing Power of Attorney for Property is a legal document in which an individual gives someone else the authority to make financial decisions on their behalf while they are capable and/or to act on their behalf in the event of mental incapacity.

Who can give a Continuing Power of Attorney for Property?

A person who gives a power of attorney is called a grantor or donor.

In order to give a Continuing Power of Attorney for Property, the grantor must be:

- 18 years or older

- mentally capable of giving a Continuing Power of Attorney for Property

A person is considered to be mentally capable of giving a Continuing Power of Attorney for Property if they:

- know what kind of property they have and its approximate value

- are aware of obligations to their dependents

- know that the attorney will be able to do anything the grantor could do if they were capable (subject to any conditions/restrictions in the Power of Attorney)

- know that the attorney must account for their management of the person's property

- know that they can revoke the Continuing Power of Attorney for Property if they are capable

- appreciate that unless the attorney does a good job of managing the property, its value may decline

- appreciate that the attorney could misuse the authority they have been given

The *Substitute Decisions Act* stipulates that the grantor and the grantee of a Continuing Power of Attorney for Property must be 18 years old because this is the age at which one is presumed to be capable of entering into contracts. This ability is necessary for someone to manage their own finances or for someone to manage another person's finances.

Who can be an Attorney for Property?

A person who acts as an attorney for property may also be referred to as the grantee or donee.

The grantee must be:

- 18 years or older (age at which people can enter into contracts)

- mentally capable of performing the duties of an attorney

- available and willing to assume responsibility for decisions

When appointing an attorney, the grantor has the option of:

- appointing one person to act as their attorney or appointing two or more attorneys to act together

- appointing another person or persons to act as an alternate in case the first attorney is unable to act when required

When two or more attorneys are appointed, they may act jointly or jointly and severally. "Jointly" means that the attorneys must always make decisions together. "Jointly and severally" means that the attorneys can make decisions together or independently of one another.

If two or more attorneys are appointed, the *Substitute Decisions Act* says they are to act jointly, unless the power of attorney states otherwise. The grantor may want to appoint two or more attorneys to act jointly so that there is greater accountability with respect to property management, but the grantor must consider how practical it will be if two or more people are required for every decision that has to be made and every cheque that has to be signed. Conversely, if appointing two or more attorneys jointly and severally, the grantor must consider the risks that may be associated with allowing the attorneys to have independent access to a bank account without consulting with each other.

What decisions can an attorney for property make?

An attorney can make any decisions related to the grantor's property and finances that the grantor could make if they were capable, except the making of a will (*Substitute Decisions Act* (section 7 (2)). An attorney for property cannot make a Power of Attorney for Personal Care for the grantor. This is a personal care decision.

An attorney for property is a person in a position of trust. The word 'fiduciary' is used to describe this person and their relationship to the grantor. Someone stands in a fiduciary relationship with regard to another person when he or she has rights and powers that must be exercised solely for the benefit of that other person. Consequently, a fiduciary is not allowed to benefit from this position beyond being paid a reasonable amount for their services. An attorney for property, as a fiduciary, may also be subject to certain common law restrictions. Investing in mutual funds or discretionary accounts involves a delegation of authority but the common law prohibits delegation for this purpose. The power of attorney needs to state the types of investments that the attorney can make if the grantor wants the attorney for property to have broader investment authority.

What are the duties of an attorney for property?

The duties of an attorney for property are listed in the *Substitute Decisions Act* (section 32) and are very specific:

- to perform their duties with honesty and integrity and in good faith for the incapable person's benefit (fiduciary duties)

- to explain to the incapable person what the duties of the attorney are

- to encourage the incapable person to participate in decision making about their property to the best of their ability

- to promote regular personal contact with the person's family and friends

- to periodically consult with supportive family, friends, and those who provide care to the incapable person

- to keep account of all transactions concerning the person's property

What are the requirements for witnessing a Continuing Power of Attorney for Property?

In order to be valid, a Continuing Power of Attorney for Property must be executed (signed) in the presence of two witnesses. Each of the two witnesses must then sign the power of attorney in the presence of each other. The *Substitute Decisions Act* (section 10) places some restrictions on who is able to witness a power of attorney. Persons who are <u>not</u> able to be witnesses include:

- the attorney or the attorney's spouse or partner

- the grantor's spouse or partner

- a child of the grantor, or a child that the grantor treats as their own child

- a person who has a guardian of property or a guardian of the person

- a person who is less than eighteen years of age

When is a Continuing Power of Attorney for Property effective?

A Continuing Power of Attorney for Property may become effective:

- while the grantor is still capable of managing property

  A Continuing Power of Attorney for Property is valid when it is prepared and executed in accordance with the *Substitute Decisions Act* and, therefore, can become effective when the grantor, while still capable, consents to its use. The Continuing Power of Attorney for Property continues to be valid even if the grantor subsequently becomes incapable of managing their property.

- when the grantor becomes incapable of managing property

If a Continuing Power of Attorney for Property states that it is only effective when the grantor becomes incapable, the grantor should indicate how and by whom their incapacity is to be determined. If these instructions are included in the Continuing Power of Attorney for Property, then it becomes effective when these conditions are met. For example, the grantor and their attorney for property may agree to leave the power of attorney document with a trusted third person such as a doctor or an accountant with instructions for the document to be given to the attorney for property when this third person has determined that the grantor is no longer mentally capable of managing property in accordance with the legal definition of mental capacity. You may indicate that a letter from this third person verifying the grantor's mental incapacity to manage property is sufficient proof for the purpose of having your attorney act. This is a type of informal assessment.

If a Continuing Power of Attorney for Property states that it is only effective when the grantor becomes incapable but does not stipulate a method for making this determination, then the power of attorney is only effective when a formal assessment by a capacity assessor has resulted in a finding of incapacity.

- at any other time or upon any other occasion that the grantor may specify

If someone has made a Continuing Power of Attorney for Property, can it be cancelled or terminated?

Yes, a Continuing Power of Attorney for Property is terminated when:

- the attorney dies, becomes incapable of managing property, or resigns

- the grantor dies

- the grantor revokes the Power of Attorney

- the grantor executes (signs and has witnessed) a new Continuing Power of Attorney for Property, unless there is a provision in the new document for multiple continuing powers of attorney

- when the court appoints a guardian of property to manage the property of the incapable person

All powers of attorney are terminated by the death of the grantor. The Estate Trustee named in a will is responsible for the financial affairs of the deceased.

How does a person revoke a Continuing Power of Attorney for Property?

A person is capable of revoking a power of attorney if they are capable of giving one. Revocation must be in writing and witnessed by the grantor and two people (*Substitute Decisions Act* (section 12(2)). The need for written revocation is based on the assumption that the document is in the hands of the attorney. In this case, the grantor will need to assure that the revocation is distributed to any third parties who might be involved with their property management; for example, banks and financial advisors.

If the power of attorney document is in the possession of the grantor and there are no copies, it would not be considered in effect and, therefore, not requiring revocation. If the grantor wanted to change the power of attorney at this point, the document could simply be destroyed and a new power of attorney executed.

As we end this chapter, **Important Things to Remember are:**

- **To appoint an attorney for property, or to be an attorney for property under a Continuing Power of Attorney for Property, a person must be 18 years or older.**

- **An attorney for property under a Continuing Power of Attorney for Property is in a position of great trust. The duties of an attorney for property are listed clearly and specifically in the *Substitute Decisions Act* (section 32).**

- **A Continuing Power of Attorney for Property may be effective while the person who gives it is capable if they request their attorney to act on their behalf.**

- **A Continuing Power of Attorney for Property continues to be effective after the person who gives it becomes incapable.**

6 Mental Capacity to Manage Property

The *Substitute Decisions Act* is the law that gives you the right to appoint an attorney for property, and it is the *Substitute Decisions Act* that tells you about mental capacity to make property decisions.

In this chapter . . .

- **when a person is incapable of managing property**

- **how mental capacity to manage property is assessed**

    ○ **formal assessment**

    ○ **informal assessment**

        ○ **when there is a Continuing Power of Attorney for Property**

        ○ **when there is no Continuing Power of Attorney for Property**

When is a person incapable of managing property?

A person is mentally incapable of managing property if the person is not able to understand information that is relevant to making a decision about their property, or is not able to appreciate the reasonably foreseeable consequences of a decision or lack of a decision (*Substitute Decisions Act* (section 6)).

A person is mentally capable of making a financial decision if they understand the nature of the financial decision and the choices that are available to them. They should be able to demonstrate an understanding of the relationship between parties to a transaction and/or the potential beneficiaries of a transaction. Most important, a person must be able to appreciate and express in his or her own words the consequences of making or not making a decision.

How is capacity to manage property assessed?

Formal assessment of capacity to manage property

When the *Substitute Decisions Act* speaks of capacity assessment and capacity assessors, the reference is to a formal method of assessment that we find in the law. These terms are often used in a generic sense for assessments done by anyone in the course of investigating another person's capacity for a specific task, but under the *Substitute Decisions Act* the terms "capacity assessor" and "capacity assessment" refer to a specific type of assessment which is conducted for specific purposes. A formal finding of incapacity to manage property may also be made under the *Mental Health Act*, but in this case the person would be a patient of a psychiatric facility and the assessment would be done by a qualified attending physician. This is not meant to diminish the importance of other types of capacity assessments which are done for other purposes, such as driving, instructing a lawyer, or marrying. These assessments may also be referred to as formal assessments and they are usually done by doctors, psychologists, social workers or other professionals who have expertise in this field. The purpose of this section of the book, however, is to focus on capacity assessment as it pertains to property and the *Substitute Decisions Act*.

Who are capacity assessors?

Capacity assessors are a select group of individuals trained by the Attorney General to do assessments of capacity under the *Substitute Decisions Act*. Capacity assessors do not play a role under the *Health Care Consent Act* and are not government employees. They are professional people who qualify to do capacity assessments because they meet certain requirements.

First, capacity assessors must be members of:

- The College of Physicians and Surgeons of Ontario,

- The College of Psychologists of Ontario,

- The College of Nurses of Ontario,

- The College of Occupational Therapists of Ontario, or

- The Ontario College of Social Workers and Social Service Workers and holding a certificate of registration for social work.

An assessor must be a member in good standing with their professional college, the body that regulates the work done in a particular profession. They are required to successfully complete a training program approved by the Attorney General and they must carry professional liability insurance. Assessors may have specialized education or experience in a particular field of work, such as dementia, schizophrenia, or head injury. The Capacity Assessment Office in Toronto has a list of assessors in each area of the province and will send the list to anyone requesting it. For more information about capacity assessment contact:

Capacity Assessment Office
c/o The Public Guardian and Trustee
595 Bay Street, 8th Floor
Toronto, ON M5G 2M6

Guidelines which an assessor must follow

An assessor must abide by certain rules when they are doing assessments. These rules are found in the *Substitute Decisions Act* (section 78). Before performing an assessment of capacity, the assessor must explain to the person:

- the purpose of the assessment

- the significance and effect of a finding of capacity or incapacity

- that the person has a right to refuse to be assessed

An assessor can only proceed with an assessment of a person's capacity if the person is not refusing to be assessed.

An assessor must complete specific assessment forms provided by the Capacity Assessment Office. These forms have been designed for the purpose of recording assessment information. An assessor who performs an assessment of a person's capacity may provide the person they have assessed with a written report of the assessor's findings.

When is a formal capacity assessment required?

A formal capacity assessment may be required:

- to arrange for or terminate a statutory guardianship of property (See Chapter 7 for more detail.)

- to arrange for or, in some cases, terminate a court-ordered guardianship

- in some cases, to make a power of attorney effective

  If the grantor requires confirmation of incapacity to manage property before the Continuing Power of Attorney for Property can come into effect but does not specify the method of capacity assessment, then the attorney is only authorized to act when they have been notified by a capacity assessor that the grantor has been assessed and found to be incapable of managing property, or the attorney is notified that a certificate of incapacity to manage property has been issued under the *Mental Health Act.*

  If the grantor requires confirmation of incapacity to manage property before the Continuing Power of Attorney for Property can come into effect, the grantor may want to specify that a formal assessment is required. However, a formal assessment of capacity by a capacity assessor for the purpose of activating a power of attorney is not a requirement of the law.

  The grantor also has the option of requesting an informal assessment to activate their power of attorney by stating how and by whom their capacity is to be determined. Informal assessment is discussed later in this chapter.

- to give or revoke a Power of Attorney for Personal Care with Special Provision(s) (See Chapter 15 for more detail.)

When is a formal capacity assessment not required?

A formal capacity assessment by a capacity assessor is not required:

- before preparing a will or Continuing Power of Attorney for Property or Power of Attorney for Personal Care, unless it is a Power of Attorney for Personal Care with Special Provisions

  If the capacity of a person to make a will or power of attorney is in question, it is wise to seek the assistance and advice of a professional person who is trained to assess capacity for that purpose. Formal assessment by a capacity assessor under the *Substitute Decisions Act* is not required.

- if there is a power of attorney in place that does not require a formal capacity assessment to become effective

- when a substitute decision maker under the *Health Care Consent Act* is authorized to make a decision

What does an assessment cost?

Assessors are not paid by the government to do assessments. Assessors work as independent contractors and it is the responsibility of the person who is requesting an assessment to pay for it. The fees that assessors charge are not regulated by the government. Rates can vary from $50./hour to $160./hour. Some assessors charge higher fees because of their expertise in a specialized field. Subsidies are available. For more information about subsidies contact the Capacity Assessment Office.

What can a person do if they disagree with a finding of incapacity?

If the person being assessed does not have a Continuing Power of Attorney for Property and is found to be incapable of managing property, a certificate of incapacity will be issued by the capacity assessor. Upon receipt of the certificate of incapacity, the Public Guardian and Trustee will become the person's statutory guardian of property. Under the *Substitute Decisions Act*, the assessed person may appeal to the Consent and Capacity Board a finding of incapacity that has resulted in statutory guardianship of property.

If the assessment is being done for the purpose of activating an existing Continuing Power of Attorney for Property and the grantor disagrees with the finding of incapacity, there is no provision for appeal to the Consent and Capacity Board under these circumstances. However, the grantor may, in some cases, still stop the attorney from acting by revoking the power of attorney. Remember that while a person may not have capacity to make property decisions, they may still have the required capacity to make or revoke a power of attorney.

Informal assessment of capacity to manage property when there is a Continuing Power of Attorney for Property

A valid Continuing Power of Attorney for Property is considered to be in effect when:

- the original, signed document is in the possession of the attorney

- the attorney, in accordance with any conditions or restrictions in the document, is acting on behalf of the grantor

Informal assessment of mental capacity does not fall to a select group of individuals. The grantor of a Continuing Power of Attorney for Property is able to include instructions about how and by whom their mental incapacity should be determined.

Some people trust the following persons to make a judgment about their capacity to manage property:

- their doctor or their lawyer

- a family member

- their attorney

An informal approach to capacity assessment can work well if the grantor:

- trusts the person who will be determining their capacity

- trusts their attorney

- is agreeable to having their attorney act on their behalf

- has a close loving family with no recent history of conflict

---

Caution: The concept of capacity and incapacity as defined in the *Substitute Decisions Act* is new and not all professionals are trained to assess capacity.

Sometimes the point at which the transfer of power from grantor to attorney should occur is not always clear. The grantor may only want the attorney to act on their behalf in the event of their mental incapacity, not realizing that the implication of this condition is that their mental capacity may be questioned, that their capacity may require assessment, and that the assessment may give rise to disagreement between the grantor and the attorney. If the release of a power of attorney is to be contingent upon an informal finding of mental incapacity, the grantor should give some direction about how and by whom their capacity is to be assessed.

John Bull is a retired doctor. He is a widower with five sons and has considerable assets. Over the years, John and his sons have all gotten along pretty well, but occasionally there have been problems. John is capable of managing his finances, but is aware that his two youngest sons have been arguing about some of John's investments. John decides to appoint his oldest son as his attorney in a Continuing Power of Attorney for Property and his second oldest son as a substitute attorney. John only wants the power of attorney to come into effect when he is no longer capable of managing his property. He discusses this with his lawyer and the power of attorney is then written with the following conditions and instructions:

- John's doctor will determine his mental capacity in accordance with the criteria found in the *Substitute Decisions Act*; and

- John's Continuing Power of Attorney for Property will be stored with the lawyer who will only release it to John's son when the doctor has verified John's mental incapacity in writing.

If the grantor includes instructions about how and by whom their incapacity to manage property should be determined for purposes of making their Continuing Power of Attorney for Property effective, their attorney has the authority to act when these conditions have been met. If the grantor doesn't agree with this informal finding of incapacity he or she may revoke the power of attorney if he or she has the capacity to do so. There is no provision for appeal to the Consent and Capacity Board in this situation.

Note: The release of the original document and the question of when an attorney begins to act can be one of the most problematic points related to the use of a power of attorney and should be tailored to meet individual needs. Ideally, if the grantor releases the document to the attorney and asks the attorney to begin acting on behalf of the grantor, then the transfer of power can occur smoothly. Often in this case, the attorney assumes more and more responsibility and eventually assumes full control of the grantor's finances once the grantor can no longer participate in the management of their property. Planning and discussion between the grantor and the attorney are important.

Wilma Klein is an 80 year old Dutch immigrant who came to live with her daughter and son-in-law five years ago. Her English is poor; she is grateful for her daughter's and son-in-law's help. At their prompting, Wilma appointed them to be her attorneys for property and did not include any conditions or restrictions. One day, Wilma received a call from the bank about some investments that had been sold. When she confronted her attorneys, they told her she was not capable of managing her finances and that they would look after her. Wilma later went to see a lawyer who found her to be capable of making a power of attorney. She revoked the existing power of attorney and appointed her grandson, Karl, in a new power of attorney. The document only permitted Karl to help with regular banking and paying bills and made his help with anything else, including investments, contingent on a finding of incapacity by Wilma's doctor. Over the next five years, Wilma's health deteriorated and Karl felt that the time had come to assume more responsibility. He took Wilma to see the doctor who referred her to a clinic that assesses capacity. The clinic reported that Wilma was not capable of managing her property and the doctor gave Karl a letter to this effect. Wilma again disagreed and went to see her lawyer. This time the lawyer found Wilma to be incapable of making, and therefore of revoking, a power of attorney for property. Karl was able to continue acting on Wilma's behalf.

Under the *Substitute Decisions Act*, a review of statutory guardianship is the only matter that can be brought to the Consent and Capacity Board. There is no provision to appeal:

- formal assessments done for the purpose of activating a power of attorney; or
- any kind of informal assessment of capacity to manage property.

Informal assessment of capacity to manage property when there is no Continuing Power of Attorney for Property

Whether a person does or does not have a Continuing Power of Attorney for Property, their incapacity to manage property is often identified in similar ways. None of us live in complete isolation. Some people are fortunate enough to have close family and friends who are in regular contact with them and who are sensitive to their physical and mental condition. Early signs of incapacity or pending incapacity may include unusual behaviour, disorientation, depression, or lack of judgment. Incapacity to manage property is most clearly identified when the consequences of poor property management become evident; for example, bills not paid or cheques not deposited. Other people live in a greater state of isolation and may not have family or friends watching out for them on a regular basis, but again, it is usually the consequences of poor property management which create a crisis in the life of an individual and draw attention to possible incapacity to manage property.

A visiting relative may sense that there is a problem and question the person's ability to look after their finances and property A neighbour may call the police if there are signs of inactivity around the person's home. A doctor may be involved if the person has health problems. These contacts tend to focus on the person's physical well being initially. Subsequently, the person's capacity to manage their property and finances may also be questioned. Everyone has financial obligations, so regardless of where someone lives or who their social contacts are, if a person is incapable of managing property it will inevitably be identified.

When someone suspects that a person is incapable of managing their property and is concerned about them, the following options might be considered:

- Talk to the alleged incapable person and see if they have or would like to find out about having a Continuing Power of Attorney for Property prepared.

- Contact local health or social service agencies such as the Community Care Access Centre, the Alzheimer Society, the Mental Health Association, etc. These agencies can provide valuable advice and/or services.

- Make an application for assessment to trigger statutory guardianship. (See Chapter 7 for more detail.)

As well as these options the *Substitute Decisions Act* (section 27) makes provision for the Public Guardian and Trustee to respond to what are called "serious adverse effects."

Serious adverse effects related to property include:

- **loss of a significant part of a person's property**
- **failure of a person to provide basic necessities of life for him or herself, or their dependents**

The Public Guardian and Trustee (PGT) must investigate any allegation that a person is incapable of managing their property and that serious adverse effects are occurring or may occur as a result. Anyone can call the PGT to report such a case, but there must be clear evidence of serious adverse effects before an investigation will be made. The PGT does not do a formal assessment of mental capacity when informed about a person who is alleged to be incapable. If, as a result of their investigation, the PGT has reason to believe that the person is incapable of managing their property, the PGT may then take further action. In order to alleviate serious adverse effects, the PGT may apply to the court to be appointed temporary guardian of property of the person who has been investigated and is believed to be incapable. This appointment as temporary guardian is effective for up to ninety days.

As we end this chapter, **Important Things to Remember are:**

- **A person is considered to be incapable of managing property when:**

  - they are not able to understand information relevant to making a property decision, and

  - they are not able to understand the reasonably foreseeable consequences of a decision or lack of decision.

- **The *Substitute Decisions Act* provides rules and requirements for a formal method of assessment by a capacity assessor.**

- **If the grantor of a Continuing Power of Attorney for Property wants the power to be contingent on a finding of incapacity, the grantor may state how and by whom their capacity is to be assessed, thus providing for an informal method of assessment.**

- **The process by which the attorney gains possession of the document and begins to act requires thoughtful planning when preparing a power of attorney.**

- **The Public Guardian and Trustee must investigate allegations that a person is suffering from serious adverse effects, which include loss of property or failure to provide the necessities of life.**

7 Property Decisions for Mentally Incapable People

The *Substitute Decisions Act* provides information about who can manage property on behalf of a person who has been assessed as being mentally incapable of managing their property.

In this chapter …

- **decision making for those who have been formally assessed under the *Substitute Decisions Act***

  o **attorney for property**

  o **statutory guardian of property**

  o **court-appointed guardian of property**

- **decision making when formal assessment is not required or has not been done**

  o **when there is an attorney for property**

  o **when there is no attorney for property**

Decision making for individuals who have been formally assessed under the *Substitute Decisions Act*

The *Substitute Decisions Act* is clear about who can make property decisions on behalf of an incapable person. (See Appendix A: Figure 2.) The following individuals can act on behalf of a person who has been formally assessed under the *Substitute Decisions Act* and found to be mentally incapable of managing their property:

- an attorney acting under a General Power of Attorney that was written prior to 1995 and has a provision in it that makes it a "continuing" power of attorney

- an attorney acting under a Continuing Power of Attorney for Property

- a statutory guardian of property

- a court-appointed guardian of property

Note: The laws governing the Old Age Pension, Canada Pension Plan, and welfare make provision for trusteeships following an assessment of incapacity. That discussion is beyond the scope of this book.

Attorney for property

Depending on how the Continuing Power of Attorney for Property is worded, there may be a requirement for formal capacity assessment before the attorney is authorized to act. This can happen in one of two ways:

- the power of attorney may state that a formal capacity assessment and finding of incapacity is required to activate the power of attorney

- the power of attorney may state that the attorney for property is only authorized to act when the grantor is incapable but the power of attorney does not state how this should be determined

Formal capacity assessment to activate a power of attorney is not a requirement of law but it is an option that some people may choose to use. If a power of attorney does not have a requirement for formal assessment, the attorney is authorized to act when they are in possession of the document and when any other conditions have been met.

Statutory guardianship of property

The word statutory means required by law. In this case, the law is the *Substitute Decisions Act* and it is this law that provides for the statutory (required by law) guardianship of an incapable person's property when there is no attorney for property. The Public Guardian and Trustee is always the first statutory guardian of property and the process by which this takes place can happen in one of two ways:

- When a capacity assessor has assessed a person and found him or her to be incapable of managing property, the assessor issues a certificate of incapacity, sending a copy to the Public Guardian and Trustee. The Public Guardian and Trustee then automatically becomes the statutory guardian of property.

- When a doctor issues a certificate under the *Mental Health Act* certifying that a person who is an in-patient of a psychiatric facility is incapable of managing property, the Public Guardian and Trustee receives a copy of the certificate and automatically becomes the statutory guardian.

> **A capacity assessor under the *Substitute Decisions Act* is a practitioner (doctor, nurse, psychologist, occupational therapist, or social worker) who has received special training approved by the Attorney General. (See Chapter 6.)**

There is no restriction on who can request a formal assessment of capacity. It can be requested by:

- a person who is suspected of being mentally incapable

- a person who suspects another person of being mentally incapable

Before a formal assessment of capacity to manage property under the *Substitute Decisions Act* is done, certain conditions must be met:

- the request has to be made on the form provided by the Capacity Assessment Office (The capacity assessor will have these.)

- anyone requesting an assessment of another person must have reason to believe that the person is mentally incapable of managing their property

- a person requesting an assessment has made reasonable inquiries and has no knowledge that there is an attorney under a Continuing Power of Attorney for Property who has authority over all the person's property

- a person requesting an assessment has made reasonable inquiries and has no knowledge of any spouse, partner or relative of the person who intends to make application for the appointment of a guardian of property for the person

If a person is assessed and found to be incapable of managing their property, the Public Guardian and Trustee will inform that person of the statutory guardianship. The Public Guardian and Trustee will explain to the person that they have the right to have the assessor's finding of incapacity reviewed. Applications to review findings of incapacity that result in statutory guardianship under the *Substitute Decisions Act* are made to the Consent and Capacity Board.

Statutory guardianship is terminated if it is found that the incapable person gave a Continuing Power of Attorney for Property that gives the attorney authority over all of the grantor's property before the certificate of incapacity was issued. The statutory guardianship may also be transferred from the Public Guardian and Trustee to another person. The *Substitute Decisions Act* (section 17 (1)) gives a list of people who can apply to replace the Public Guardian and Trustee as an incapable person's statutory guardian of property:

- the incapable person's spouse or partner

- a relative of the incapable person

- the incapable person's attorney under a continuing power of attorney for property (if the power of attorney was made before the certificate of incapacity was issued and does not give the attorney authority over all of the incapable person's property)

- a trust corporation (if the incapable person's spouse or partner is not willing or able to act on behalf of the incapable person and if the spouse or partner consents in writing to a trust corporation managing the incapable person's property)

Through statutory guardianship, the law makes provision for the management of an incapable person's property where no attorney for property has been appointed. The Public Guardian and Trustee sees itself as the decision maker of last resort and every effort is made to find family who are willing and able to assume the role of statutory guardian.

By being the first statutory guardian of property, the Public Guardian and Trustee ensures that the person who applies to replace the Public Guardian and Trustee is capable of managing property and that they understand their responsibilities. Statutory guardianship encourages family involvement, while at the same time protecting those who are vulnerable and/or those who have no family to act on their behalf.

It is important not to ignore the signs that someone may be having difficulty managing their property. Even though the person may be incapable of managing their property, they may still be capable of giving a Continuing Power of Attorney for Property. Often, when the early signs of difficulty are recognized, the person who is affected is agreeable to having a family member or friend act as their attorney. Action at this point can avoid the need to apply for statutory guardianship or court-appointed guardianship later.

Sam Gonzales is a 47 year old man of Spanish descent who has lived at the Grayson Boarding Home for almost 10 years. Sam was diagnosed with schizophrenia when he was twenty and has other medical problems including diabetes and bronchitis. He receives a disability pension and over the years, Mary Grayson, the owner of the Boarding Home, has periodically helped Sam with his finances during his periods of disorientation. Sam trusts Mary, but they have never talked about powers of attorney. Recently Sam has begun to exhibit difficult behaviour and has not been paying his bills. Mary thinks that Sam has a sister, but she has never come to visit Sam. Not knowing what to do, Mary called a lawyer who agreed to see Sam. Even though Sam is having difficulty managing his finances, the lawyer found Sam to be capable of giving a power of attorney. With Mary's agreement, Sam appoints her to be his attorney for property in a Continuing Power of Attorney for Property.

In the case of Sam Gonzales, if a formal assessment of Sam's ability to manage his property had been done and Sam had been assessed as mentally incapable of managing his property, the Public Guardian and Trustee (PGT) would have been notified and would have automatically become Sam's statutory guardian. The PGT would have made every effort to find Sam's sister and evaluate her ability and willingness to replace the PGT as statutory guardian. If the sister could not be found or if she was unwilling to replace the PGT as Sam's statutory guardian, the PGT would have to continue to act on Sam's behalf. It is not possible for a friend, such as Sam's friend Mary, to replace the PGT as statutory guardian.

Court-appointed guardianship of property

Any person can apply to a court to have a guardian of property appointed for a person who is incapable of managing property if it is necessary for decisions to be made on the incapable person's behalf (*Substitute Decisions Act* (section 22(1)). Once guardianship has been granted, it can only be terminated by a further judicial application or motion.

Court-appointed guardianship is invasive and the process for obtaining it is usually stressful and expensive. The provisions that the *Substitute Decisions Act* makes for attorneys and statutory guardians address the needs of most individuals. Court-appointed guardianship occurs infrequently and should be viewed as a last resort where other measures do not adequately address the needs and best interests of an incapable person.

It is beyond the scope of this book to discuss further applications for court-appointed guardianship. For more information, the reader should refer to the *Substitute Decisions Act* (sections 22-40 and Part III) or call the office of the Public Guardian and Trustee.

Decision making when formal assessment is not required or has not been done

When there is an attorney for property

A power of attorney is a powerful document and this is why it is so important for the grantor to trust the attorney. When a person has appointed an attorney for property in a Continuing Power of Attorney for Property and the document does not require any conditions to be met before it can be used, the attorney has authority to make decisions when they are in possession of the document. The attorney will be able to do almost everything with the grantor's property that the grantor is able to do. This is why some attorneys run into difficulty dealing with banks and other third parties when they begin to act on behalf of the grantor. Even though there is no legal requirement for the attorney to prove that the grantor wants help at this time, some banks will request some kind of confirmation that the grantor is incapable and/or that the grantor wants the attorney to act. This can add more stress to an already difficult situation but the request is seen by banks as good practice and is done to protect the interests of their client, the grantor. The transition from the grantor to the attorney can occur more smoothly if the attorney begins to assist the grantor before he or she becomes incapable. It is a good idea for the attorney to have an overview of the grantor's finances and to meet with the staff at the various financial institutions. A gradual transition can build trust among all who are involved.

When there is no attorney for property

The *Substitute Decisions Act* does <u>not</u> provide a list of substitute decision makers for property similar to the list that we find for health care. Some people think that family or friends will be able to act on their behalf if the need should arise, but this is not the case.

If a person chooses not to appoint an attorney for property and the person becomes incapable of managing property there is always the risk that he or she could suffer loss at the hand of an unscrupulous person. The ways to help someone in this position are limited.

First, even though the person may have lost their capacity to manage property, it's important to see if the person is still capable of appointing an attorney for property. A person is free to choose anyone 18 years of age or older to be their attorney. The attorney must be trusted and should not be anyone whose motives or ability are in question. A trust company can act as an attorney and this may be an option for some people to consider. The Public Guardian and Trustee (PGT) cannot be appointed as an attorney unless the PGT agrees in advance and in writing. It is unlikely that the PGT will agree to be named as attorney unless the person is incapable and has no one else to name.

Claire St.Amant lives alone in the farmhouse that she grew up in. She is 55 years old, suffers from multiple sclerosis and periodic bouts of depression. With the support of community agencies and her disability pension she seemed to be managing until recently. Workers going into the home noticed that she was losing weight and becoming more depressed. Unopened mail was piling up and bills were left unpaid but most troublesome was her changed behaviour and refusal to accept help. The Meals on Wheels coordinator was afraid that Claire was not eating at all and that her physical condition was deteriorating. The Community Care Access Centre called a case conference to decide how best to help Claire. The case manager knew that Claire had a brother living in the area but she had never appointed an attorney for property or personal care. One suggestion was to call the Public Guardian and Trustee to investigate serious adverse effects but there was concern about the time that this would take. The case manager contacted Claire's doctor and provided information from the conference. Being aware of her history and having seen Claire recently, the doctor decided to admit her on a Form 1 for assessment and regulation of her medications. A short hospital stay might restore her to her previous level of functioning and then, once at home again, the social worker could discuss and help Claire prepare powers of attorney. All agreed that this would support Claire's own goal of living independently at home.

Health and social service agencies such as the Community Care Access Centre, the Alzheimer Society, Multiple Sclerosis Society, mental health agencies, and others can provide valuable advice and guidance. These agencies may already be familiar with the person and may be providing support in the form of personal care services. They are familiar with the procedures that are available under different laws to assist someone who is incapable and doesn't have an attorney for property. Statutory guardianship or the investigation of serious adverse effects may be required. Sometimes procedures under the *Mental Health Act* may be appropriate and necessary.

As we end this chapter, **Important Things to Remember are:**

- **If a person is assessed and found to be incapable of managing property, individuals who can manage property on their behalf are:**

  - **an attorney for property**
  - **a statutory guardian of property**
  - **a court-appointed guardian of property**

- **If it is necessary, the Public Guardian and Trustee is the first statutory guardian and can be replaced by one or more members of the incapable person's family.**

- **The Public Guardian and Trustee encourages family involvement and considers itself to be the decision maker of last resort.**

- **If the grantor has appointed an attorney for property and the power of attorney document doesn't contain any conditions or restrictions, then the attorney has the authority to act when the attorney is in possession of the original signed document.**

- **The options for helping someone who is incapable and doesn't have an attorney for property are limited and may require formal procedures under the *Substitute Decisions Act* or the *Mental Health Act.***

8 Your Decision to Make a Continuing Power of Attorney for Property

One of the best reasons to appoint an attorney in a Continuing Power of Attorney for Property is to avoid having the Public Guardian and Trustee become your statutory guardian.

In this chapter

- **reasons for appointing an attorney for property**

  - **to avoid statutory guardianship**

  - **if you are married**

  - **if you are not married**

  - **if you are living with a disease that can lead to incapacity**

- **preparation of a Continuing Power of Attorney for Property**

  - **conditions and restrictions**

  - **other clauses to consider**

All of the information discussed thus far in this part has focused on your right to appoint someone as an attorney for property and the legal processes that govern that relationship. The question of whether you personally should appoint an attorney for property still remains.

Reasons for appointing an attorney for property

To avoid statutory guardianship

Whether mentally capable or incapable, every person has financial decisions that need to be made. Because of this need, the *Substitute Decisions Act* has been written to accommodate the possibility that people may not have an attorney for property. The provision for statutory guardianship acts as a safeguard:

- to ensure that the incapable person's property is protected by making the Public Guardian and Trustee the first statutory guardian while there is no one else who can legally make property decisions on the incapable person's behalf

- to enable family to apply for and replace the Public Guardian and Trustee as statutory guardian

- to enable the Public Guardian and Trustee, as a last resort, to continue to act as guardian for an incapable person when there is no one else to step in and make property decisions on the incapable person's behalf.

Remember, you can appoint a friend, business associate or anyone you choose to be your attorney for property, but if you are ever assessed as being mentally incapable and do not have an attorney for property, only family members can apply to replace the Public Guardian and Trustee and become your statutory guardian. If you choose not to appoint an attorney for property, who in your family is most likely to help you look after your financial affairs and/or apply to become your statutory guardian if you become mentally incapable?

If you are ever assessed and found to be mentally incapable of managing your property and do not have an attorney for property, the Public Guardian and Trustee may become your statutory guardian. One of the best reasons for appointing an attorney in a Continuing Power of Attorney for Property is to avoid having the Public Guardian and Trustee become your statutory guardian.

If you are married

Many people assume that if they became incapable their spouse or partner would be able to act on their behalf. Where there is joint ownership of assets or bank accounts, the ability for basic financial affairs to be managed temporarily without applying for guardianship is certainly possible. However, certain aspects of property management cannot be managed without an attorney for property or guardian; for example, filing tax returns, making certain investments and, if you are married and own your family's home or condominium, the selling or refinancing of the home. In the latter case, the signatures of both spouses are necessary even if the home is in one spouse's name alone. Therefore, if one spouse became incapable and had not given the other spouse power of attorney, he or she would have to apply to the Public Guardian and Trustee to be given the authority to sign the deed or mortgage documents on behalf of the incapable spouse. If you are married and own a family home, it is a particularly good idea to appoint an attorney for property.

Joe and Lorraine Delutek both had jobs at a local cosmetics factory. One night while driving home from the afternoon shift Joe fell asleep, drove off the road and suffered a head injury. Five months later Joe was still in a coma. With the family income reduced, Lorraine struggled to make ends meet for herself and her eight year old son. There was a small amount of equity in their home but when Lorraine talked to the bank manager she learned that because she and Joe had not named each other as attorney for property in a Continuing Power of Attorney for Property, she could not sell or refinance the home without his signature. Not being able to make the mortgage payments any longer, Lorraine decided the easiest thing to do was just pack up their belongings and leave.

If you are not married

If you are single, widowed, separated or divorced who would make property decisions for you in the absence of an attorney for property? If a formal assessment of your capacity resulted in statutory guardianship who might be appointed to replace the Public Guardian and Trustee as your statutory guardian? Are there family members whom you would not want making property decisions for you? Is it possible that two or more family members might dispute their right to act on your behalf or might disagree about certain property decisions? Do you have a close friend whom you would choose over a family member? If any of these is the case, then you should appoint an attorney in a Continuing Power of Attorney for Property.

When mental incapacity occurs

In situations where mental incapacity can be anticipated, such as chronic or terminal illness, dementia, or mental health problems, the appointment of an attorney for property should be considered early on. This gives you the opportunity to consider the selection of an attorney and to discuss your plans, wishes and instructions with your chosen attorney. Once your capacity begins to decrease, your attorney for property can assist you to participate in decision making to the extent that you are able.

In situations where mental incapacity occurs and has not been anticipated, such as a stroke or a head injury from a car accident, the lack of an attorney for property causes added anxiety for family members who are already under significant stress as a result of the crisis. Without a power of attorney, someone in your family would have to apply to the Public Guardian and Trustee, fill out forms and prove that they would be an appropriate statutory guardian. If you become mentally incapable, have dependents, or operate a business, it is reassuring to know that an attorney for property under a Continuing Power of Attorney for Property can simply step in and act on your behalf if necessary.

Preparing a Continuing Power of Attorney for Property

Our ability to make our own decisions is a right that we hold sacred. We don't want to think about the possibility that we might ever become mentally incapable and lose our decision making independence. We neglect to plan for the future and, as a result, relatively few people have a Continuing Power of Attorney for Property. Those that do tend to be older people, even though the need for a power of attorney is not age related.

Jack Huang is a 38 year old man who lives in Richmond Hill, ON, with his wife, Sue Lyn and family. Jack owns two local restaurants and has done well in business. He owns a house and has a cottage property on Lake Muskoka. His other assets include a $200,000. life insurance policy, RRSP's, stocks, and bonds. Jack has also been contributing to a Registered Education Savings Plan for his two children. Tam, his son, is still in high school, and Lily, the oldest, has just started university. After all these years Jack and Sue Lyn are just now getting around to making wills and powers of attorney. As they meet with the lawyer they realize that there is a lot going on in their lives financially. The lawyer talks to them about their needs and about clauses that are important when you own a home and a business, and have a variety of investments. It gives them peace of mind to know that if either or both of them died or became mentally incapable they now have a plan and the required documents to help their family through such a crisis.

Jack Huang's grandmother, Edna, also lives with the Huang family. Edna is 83 years old. She has a few GIC's and mostly depends on her government pensions to cover her expenses. She pays Jack $1,000. per month for room and board, leaving her with about $200. per month for clothes and spending money. Jack takes good care of his grandmother and Edna trusts him and wants him to look after her finances. Jack obtained a power of attorney kit from the local MPP's office. Edna fills it out, appointing Jack as her attorney for property and personal care. She appoints her granddaughter Lily as an alternate and doesn't include any conditions or restrictions. Jack asks the neighbours next door to be witnesses when Edna signs.

Many people have the impression that the preparation of powers of attorney is something that should be done when we are older. If we pause to think about our assets and all the financial decisions that we make, there is usually a lot more financial activity when we are young or middle aged adults than when we become very elderly.

A Continuing Power of Attorney for Property does not have to be written in any specific form. The requirements for a valid document are few and include:

- a grantor who is capable of granting the power

- a named attorney or attorneys

- a statement giving the attorney power to make property decisions on the grantor's behalf

- the grantor's signature

- the date

- the signatures of two qualifying witnesses

The requirements related to the preparation and use of a Continuing Power of Attorney for Property were discussed in Chapter 5. A well drafted document reflects the specific needs of the grantor. It may be simple or detailed. If conditions and/or restrictions are included the grantor should be made aware of the implications that these may have. When preparing a power of attorney for property it is wise to work with a professional who can provide advice about these and other clauses that address the grantor's life situation.

Conditions and Restrictions

A condition is a requirement that must be met before your attorney for property can act. Conditions requiring the assessment of a grantor's capacity and confirmation of incapacity before the attorney can act were discussed in Chapter 6. In other conditions the grantor may include a requirement that the attorney consult with certain family members or advisors before making certain decisions.

A restriction means that a limitation has been placed on the authority of the attorney. Some grantors may want to limit the activity of the attorney to certain areas, such as management of income and spending. Some grantors may want to restrict the attorney from managing certain assets, such as real estate or investments. There may be a specification of certain people with regard to loans or gifts.

Care is needed if you choose to limit your attorney's authority. Even though you have appointed an attorney for property, if you become mentally incapable and have limited their authority, it may be necessary for someone to apply for guardianship in order to manage the balance of your property. If this happens, a management plan must be filed and security may be required. Think carefully before including conditions or restrictions related to property management.

Other clauses to consider

A power of attorney for property can be written simply with little detail or it may contain detailed clauses to address the specific needs and concerns of the grantor. Clauses that the grantor may want to consider include:

- compensation of the attorney
- the use of multiple powers of attorney
- types of investments the attorney is authorized to make
- *Family Law Act* provisions regarding interests in the matrimonial home
- a method for resolving disputes if there is more than one attorney

Remember, a Continuing Power of Attorney for Property is a very powerful document. The rules about giving this power include the need for the grantor to understand that the value of their property may decline if not managed prudently and that it is possible for the attorney to misuse the power given to them. You must be able to trust the person that you appoint in a power of attorney. Should you appoint an attorney in a Continuing Power of Attorney for Property? For most people, the answer is "yes", but the document should always be prepared with thoughtful consideration and with full knowledge of its implications.

As we end this chapter, **Important Things to Remember** are:

- **When considering whether to prepare a Continuing Power of Attorney for Property:**

  - **Be an informed consumer. Don't just sign standard forms without reviewing your life situation and understanding what you need.**

  - **Ask questions and get help. Understand why the document is important to you and what it does for you.**

  - **Choose an attorney in whom you have complete trust and confidence.**

  - **Remember that you may never have to use the power of attorney that you make, but if you do, you are the one who benefits or is adversely affected by the choices you have made.**

Part III
Power of Attorney for Personal Care

9 Rules and Requirements related to Powers of Attorney for Personal Care

A Power of Attorney for Personal Care is a legal document in which an individual gives another person the authority to make personal care decisions on their behalf if they become incapable of making personal care decisions.

In this chapter ...

- **who can give a Power of Attorney for Personal Care**

- **who can be an attorney for personal care**

- **what decisions an attorney for personal care can make**

- **the duties of an attorney for personal care**

- **the requirements for witnessing a Power of Attorney for Personal Care**

- **when a Power of Attorney for Personal Care is effective**

- **cancelling, terminating, or revoking a Power of Attorney for Personal Care**

The decisions that an attorney for personal care may be asked to make are much more intimate than paying the hydro bill or renewing GIC's. If you appoint someone to be your attorney for personal care, they must be trustworthy, but they must also have the integrity to consider your beliefs and values when they make a decision. They must be able to step outside of their own system of values and make decisions that you would want, whether they personally agree with them or not. This is different from the attorney for property whose objectives in managing your property may be somewhat consistent with the way they would manage their own property.

The questions asked in Chapter 5 about the Continuing Power of Attorney for Property are now asked here in relation to the Power of Attorney for Personal Care. Although there are some similarities, you should begin to see and understand some of the differences as you compare the two.

What is a Power of Attorney for Personal Care ?

A Power of Attorney for Personal Care is a legal document in which an individual gives another person the authority to make personal care decisions on the their behalf if they become incapable of making their own personal care decisions.

Who can give a Power of Attorney for Personal Care ?

A person who gives a Power of Attorney for Personal Care is called a 'grantor' or 'donor'.

In order to give a Power of Attorney for Personal Care the grantor must be:

- 16 years or older

- mentally capable of giving a Power of Attorney for Personal Care

A person is considered to be mentally capable of giving a Power of Attorney for Personal Care if:

- they understand that the person they have selected as their attorney has a genuine concern for their welfare

- they understand that their attorney may have to make decisions for them (*Substitute Decisions Act* (section 47.1))

Who can be an attorney for personal care?

A person who acts as an Attorney for Personal Care may also be referred to as the 'grantee' or 'donee'.

The grantee must be:

- 16 years or older (unless he or she is the incapable person's parent)

- mentally capable of performing the duties of an attorney

- available and willing to assume responsibility for decisions

- not prohibited by court order or separation agreement from having access to the incapable person

When appointing an attorney, the grantor has the option of:

- appointing one person to act as their attorney or appointing two or more attorneys to act together

- appointing another person or persons to act as an alternate in case the first attorney is unable to act when required.

When two or more attorneys are appointed, they may act jointly or jointly and severally.

"Jointly and severally" means that the attorneys can make decisions together or independently of one another.

"Jointly" means that the attorneys must always make decisions together.

If two or more attorneys are appointed, the *Substitute Decisions Act* says they are to act jointly unless the power of attorney states otherwise.

Who cannot be an attorney for personal care?

A person cannot act as an attorney under a Power of Attorney for Personal Care if:

- he or she provides health care to the grantor for compensation (unless the proposed attorney is the grantor's spouse, partner or relative)

- he or she provides residential, social, training or support services for compensation (unless the proposed attorney is the grantor's spouse, partner or relative) (*Substitute Decisions Act* (section 46.3))

What decisions can an attorney for personal care make?

An attorney for personal care makes personal care decisions that include:

- health care (which includes medical treatments)
- nutrition
- shelter
- clothing
- hygiene
- safety

A Power of Attorney for Personal Care may limit the attorney's authority to any one of the areas listed above or it may be general and give authority for decisions in all of the areas listed. An attorney can only make decisions if the power of attorney document gives them authority for that particular area. A Power of Attorney for Personal Care may include instructions or wishes about how certain decisions are to be made. Instructions may also be written in a separate document such as a Living Will or Advance Health Care Directive, or the instructions and wishes may be expressed orally. To the best of their ability, the attorney for personal care has a legal duty to follow wishes and instructions given by the grantor.

What are the duties of an attorney for personal care?

An attorney for personal care makes personal care decisions (as specified in the Power of Attorney for Personal Care) if and when the grantor becomes incapable. The attorney must follow the most recently expressed wishes and instructions, written or oral, which the grantor gave while they were still capable. If the instructions are not clear then the attorney must act in the best interests of the grantor. In determining the best interests of the grantor, the attorney must consider the grantor's beliefs and values, current wishes if they can be ascertained, and how the decision will affect the quality of the grantor's life.

The duties of an attorney for personal care are listed in the *Substitute Decisions Act* (section 66) and are very specific:

- to perform their duties diligently and in good faith for the incapable person's benefit

- to explain to the incapable person what the duties of the attorney are

- to encourage the incapable person to participate in decision making about their personal care to the best of their ability

- to promote regular personal contact with the person's family and friends

- to periodically consult with supportive family, friends and those who provide care to the incapable person

- to keep account of all transactions concerning the incapable person's personal care

- to promote the independence of the person as far as possible

- to choose the least restrictive and intrusive course of action that is available and appropriate to the situation.

What are the requirements for witnessing a Power of Attorney for Personal Care?

In order to be valid, a Power of Attorney for Personal Care must be executed (signed) in the presence of two witnesses. Each of the two witnesses must then sign the power of attorney in the presence of one another. The *Substitute Decisions Act* (section 10) places some restrictions on who is able to witness a power of attorney.

Persons who are not able to be witnesses include:

- the grantor's spouse or partner

- the attorney or the attorney's spouse or partner

- a child of the grantor, or a child that the grantor treats as their own child

- a person who has a guardian of property or a guardian of the person

- a person who is less than eighteen years of age

When is a Power of Attorney for Personal Care effective?

A Power of Attorney for Personal Care is only effective when the grantor becomes incapable of making their own personal care decisions. The determination of mental capacity to make personal care decisions is discussed in Chapters 10 and 11.

If someone has made a Power of Attorney for Personal Care, can it be cancelled or terminated?

Yes, a Power of Attorney for Personal Care is terminated when:

- the attorney dies, becomes incapable of their own personal care, or resigns

- the grantor dies

- when the grantor revokes the Power of Attorney

- when the grantor executes (signs and has witnessed) a new Power of Attorney for Personal Care, unless the old power of attorney makes a provision for multiple powers of attorney for personal care

- when the court appoints a guardian of the person to make personal care decisions on behalf of the incapable person. (*Substitute Decisions Act* (section 12))

All powers of the attorney are terminated by the death of the grantor. The Estate Trustee named in a will is responsible for most personal care decisions that might be required after death such as funeral arrangements. Your closest next-of-kin is responsible for making decisions about organ donation and donation of your body for medical education and research.

How does a person revoke a Power of Attorney for Personal Care?

A person is capable of revoking a Power of Attorney for Personal Care if they are capable of giving one. The revocation of a power of attorney must be in writing, signed by the grantor, and witnessed by two people (*Substitute Decisions Act* (section 12)).

The need for written revocation is based on the assumption that the document is in the hands of the attorney. In this case, the grantor will need to assure that the revocation is distributed to any third parties who might be involved with their personal care; for example, a physician or a nurse.

If the power of attorney document is in the possession of the grantor and there are no copies, the document would not be considered in effect and therefore not requiring revocation. If the grantor wanted to change the power of attorney at this point, the document could simply be destroyed and a new power of attorney executed.

As we end this chapter, **Important Things to Remember are:**

- **To appoint an attorney for personal care or to be an attorney for personal care under a Power of Attorney for Personal Care you must be 16 years or older.**

- **Personal Care decisions include health care, nutrition, shelter, clothing, hygiene, and safety.**

- **An attorney for personal care has a legal duty to follow the most recently expressed wishes and instructions, oral and written, of the grantor.**

- **Instructions may also be found in the Power of Attorney for Personal Care, or in other documents such as an Advance Health Care Directive or Living Will.**

- **A Power of Attorney for Personal Care only comes into effect when the grantor is no longer capable of making their own personal care decisions.**

10 Personal Care Decision Making Under the Health Care Consent Act

The *Health Care Consent Act* provides for the assessment of mental capacity and decision making with respect to treatment, admission to a care facility and provision of personal assistance services.

In this chapter ...

- **mental capacity and decision making related to treatment decisions**

- **mental capacity and decision making related to admission to a care facility**

- **mental capacity and decision making related to personal assistance services**

The purpose of the *Health Care Consent Act* is to provide rules about giving and refusing consent to treatment, admission to a Long Term Care facility and personal assistance services in a Long Term Care facility. With respect to these decisions the Act supports independent decision making by allowing those who have been found to be incapable to apply to the Consent and Capacity Board for a review of the finding; by allowing incapable persons to request that the Board appoint a representative of the person's choice for the purpose of making decisions on their behalf; and by requiring that wishes expressed by persons while capable be followed, if possible. The Act attempts to promote communication and understanding between health practitioners and their patients or clients. It ensures a significant role for supportive family members when a person lacks the capacity to make a decision. It permits intervention by the Public Guardian and Trustee only when there is no other substitute or when two or more substitutes cannot come to an agreement.

Treatment Decisions

Determining mental capacity to make a treatment decision

Treatment, as defined in the *Health Care Consent Act,* includes anything that is done for a therapeutic, preventive, palliative, diagnostic, cosmetic or other health related purpose, including a course of treatment or plan of treatment.

Treatment does not include assessment of capacity, general assessment of a person's condition, taking of a health history, communication of a diagnosis, admission to a hospital, personal assistance services, or treatment that under the circumstances poses little or no risk.

A health practitioner is someone who provides health services to people. Any working health practitioner in Ontario must be a member of their professional College. These are the organizations that regulate and set standards for the profession and include:

- the College of Audiologists and Speech-Language Pathologists of Ontario
- the College of Chiropodists of Ontario (including a member who is a podiatrist)
- the College of Chiropractors of Ontario
- the College of Dental Hygienists of Ontario
- the Royal College of Dental Surgeons of Ontario
- the College of Denturists of Ontario
- the College of Dietitians of Ontario
- the College of Massage Therapists of Ontario
- the College of Medical Laboratory Technologists of Ontario
- the College of Medical Radiation Technologists of Ontario
- the College of Midwives of Ontario
- the College of Nurses of Ontario

- the College of Occupational Therapists of Ontario
- the College of Optometrists of Ontario
- the College of Physicians and Surgeons of Ontario
- the College of Physiotherapists of Ontario
- the College of Psychologists of Ontario
- the College of Respiratory Therapists of Ontario
- the Ontario College of Social Workers and Social Service Workers, regulating those social workers who hold a certificate of registration for social work

A naturopath registered as a drugless therapist under the *Drugless Practitioners Act* is also a health practitioner.

Any health practitioner who is proposing a treatment for someone else must first obtain the consent (expressed or implied) of that person. For consent to treatment to be valid, the consent must:

- relate to the treatment

- be informed

- be given voluntarily

- not be obtained through misrepresentation or fraud

For consent to treatment to be informed, a person should expect to receive the following information from a health practitioner:

- the nature of the treatment

- the expected benefits of the treatment

- the material risks of the treatment

- the material side effects of the treatment

- alternative courses of action

- the likely consequences of not having the treatment

A person should also be given the opportunity to have their questions answered by the health practitioner with respect to the proposed treatment.

A health practitioner has a legal duty to obtain informed consent for any treatment that they are proposing. Determining whether a person is mentally capable of making a treatment decision is a necessary part of obtaining the person's consent for that treatment. Section 4 of the *Health Care Consent Act* defines capacity as follows:

A person is mentally capable to make decisions about treatment, admission to a Long Term Care facility or personal assistance services, if they:

- understand the information that is relevant to making a decision

- appreciate the reasonably foreseeable consequences of a decision or lack of a decision

If the health practitioner believes that the person is mentally incapable of making a decision or of giving consent to a proposed treatment, then the health practitioner must seek the consent of that person's substitute decision maker. As well, the health practitioner, in accordance with the health practitioner's College guidelines, must inform the person of his or her right to make application to the Consent and Capacity Board for a review of the finding of incapacity.

Who makes treatment decisions for a person who is mentally incapable?

Giving or refusing consent to treatment is probably the most common personal care decision that any of us make. Because some people will not have prepared a Power of Attorney for Personal Care, the law accommodates a decision making process that identifies a decision maker other than an attorney. Sometimes incapacity can be anticipated, but sometimes it happens quickly and without warning, as in the case of a car accident or a stroke. If an incapable person has not appointed an attorney for personal care and a treatment decision is required, a health practitioner needs to be able to contact a substitute decision maker who can give or refuse consent without delay. (See Appendix A: Figure 4.)

The *Health Care Consent Act* provides a list of substitute decision makers who are able to give or refuse consent to treatment for an incapable person. The list is given in order of authority. In other words, a substitute decision maker is selected because there is no one else above them on the list with greater authority who is willing and able to make the decision.

The following list from section 20 of the *Health Care Consent Act* is sometimes referred to as the hierarchy of substitute decision makers:

- the incapable person's guardian of the person

- the incapable person's attorney for personal care

- the incapable person's representative appointed by the Consent and Capacity Board

- the incapable person's spouse or partner

- a child or parent of the incapable person

- a parent of an incapable person who has only a right of access

- a brother or sister of the incapable person

- any other relative of the incapable person

There may be two or more persons in any of the above groups who qualify to be substitute decision makers and who disagree about whether to give or refuse consent. If they cannot agree, the Public Guardian and Trustee may be called to make the decision in their place. The Public Guardian and Trustee is also the decision maker of last resort when there is no person on the list who meets the requirements to be a decision maker.

To be a substitute decision maker one must be 16 years old, unless they are the parent of the incapable person. The substitute decision maker must be mentally capable with respect to the treatment and must not be prohibited by court order or separation agreement from giving or refusing consent on the incapable person's behalf or from having access to the incapable person. The substitute decision maker must also be available and willing to assume responsibility for making the decision. A substitute decision maker who makes a decision concerning a treatment on behalf of an incapable person shall do so in accordance with any wishes that the person expressed while still capable. If the substitute decision maker doesn't know of any wishes or if it is impossible to comply with the wish, the substitute decision maker shall make the decision in the person's best interests (*Health Care Consent Act* (section 21)). In deciding what the best interests of the person are, the substitute decision maker should consider:

- the beliefs and values that the incapable person held while capable and would still be likely to act on

- whether the incapable person's condition is likely to improve, remain the same or deteriorate without the treatment

- whether the benefit of the treatment outweighs any risk of harm to the person

- whether a less restrictive or less intrusive treatment would be as beneficial as the one being proposed

Leonard Copegog and his wife, Berdette, are Anishinabek of the Beausoleil First Nation band. The live in a small house on Christian Island with Leonard's son, his wife and four children. Leonard has been diabetic for ten years and six months ago he had a stroke. He is aphasic but Berdette feels he understands what she is saying. Recently, the ulcers on Leonard's right foot have become gangrenous and the doctor is recommending a below knee amputation. Leonard is incapable of making the decision and the doctor looks to Berdette as his substitute decision maker. The doctor meets twice with Berdette to explain Leonard's condition and the need for surgery but Berdette refuses to give consent because she is afraid that Leonard will be sent to a nursing home. The doctor considers applying to the Consent and Capacity Board because Berdette's refusal to give consent is not in Leonard's best interest but after further consideration he chooses another approach. The doctor determines that Berdette is incapable of making this decision because she does not appreciate the life threatening nature of Leonard's condition. The doctor informs Berdette that he finds her to be incapable of making the decision and Berdette does not wish to challenge this. The doctor now looks to Leonard's son, the next highest ranking substitute decision maker, to make the decision.

This story underlines the importance of determining whether the incapable person's substitute decision maker is capable of making the treatment decision. If not, the health practitioner can inform the substitute of a finding of incapacity, explain his or her right of appeal and, in the absence of an appeal, move on to the next substitute decision maker.

The story, however, doesn't necessarily end there. Leonard's son may be capable of making the decision but that doesn't mean he will give consent for amputation. There may be cultural factors affecting the son's decision or, because of Leonard's long history of diabetes and problem with ulcers, Leonard and his son may have discussed this potential scenario before Leonard had the stroke. If Leonard's son refused to give consent and the health practitioner strongly disagreed, the health practitioner could make application to the Consent and Capacity Board for a determination of whether the substitute decision maker was acting according to the principles for substitute decision making. If, on the other hand, Leonard's son felt the circumstances had changed and that he wanted to give consent contrary to what his father wanted, Leonard's son could apply to the Consent and Capacity Board for permission to depart from the previous wishes of his father. A treatment decision is not always easy. Besides understanding information about the treatment, the decision requires consideration of the person's beliefs, values and wishes; cultural factors and future quality of life.

Admission to a Long Term Care facility

Determining mental capacity to consent to admission

Admission to a Long Term Care facility is a health care decision. The definition of 'care facility' in the *Health Care Consent Act* includes those institutions that are commonly known as Homes for the Aged and Nursing Homes. Waiting lists and admissions to these publicly funded Long Term Care facilities are managed by your local Community Care Access Centre. The *Health Care Consent Act* outlines a process for admission to a Long Term Care facility which is intended to ensure that the person applying for admission is consenting to the admission if they are capable, or that the substitute decision maker is giving consent if the person is mentally incapable.

Note: Admission to government subsidized supportive housing units or to privately owned and operated retirement homes is a personal care (shelter) decision which is governed by the *Substitute Decisions Act*.

It seems reasonable that a health practitioner who is proposing a treatment for someone would give the person the information that they need to make a decision, and then, would only proceed with the treatment after consent has been obtained. But what about admission to a Long Term Care facility? When admission to a Long Term Care facility is proposed, who decides whether the person is capable of making that decision? Decision making about shelter is quite different than giving or refusing consent to treatment. The *Health Care Consent Act* says that an evaluator must determine whether a person is capable of consenting to admission to a Long Term Care facility.

An evaluator is a health practitioner who is a member of one of the following professional Colleges:

   _ the College of Audiologists and Speech-Language Pathologists of Ontario
   _ the College of Nurses of Ontario
   _ the College of Occupational Therapists of Ontario
   _ the College of Physicians and Surgeons of Ontario
   _ the College of Physiotherapists of Ontario
   _ the College of Psychologists of Ontario
   _ the Ontario College of Social Workers and Social Service Workers, and holding a certificate of registration for social work

All applications for admission (placement) to a Long Term Care facility are handled by staff of the Community Care Access Centre (CCAC) and part of their job is to guide people through the process of assessment and capacity determination. Often family members call the CCAC to enquire about placement for someone in their family. CCAC staff will want to know whether the person is aware of the call and whether they want to be admitted to a Long Term Care facility.

If the person and/or their family want to proceed with placement after talking to CCAC staff, the next step is for CCAC staff to assess the care needs of the person. Because the CCAC is the link between the Long Term Care facility and the person being admitted, CCAC staff collect medical, physical, and social information that is passed on to the Long Term Care facility. Through this assessment process, a person's mental capacity to consent to admission to a Long Term Care facility is determined.

Any health practitioner who qualifies to be an evaluator and who is providing the CCAC with assessment information may be asked by CCAC staff to determine the applicant's capacity. If a person is in hospital, it could be the nurse/discharge planner who determines capacity. If a person is receiving services at home, it could be the nurse or therapist who determines capacity. If a person is living in a retirement home, it could be the nurse on staff or a social worker in the community who determines capacity.

Who gives consent for admission for a person who is mentally incapable?

If a person is mentally incapable, Community Care Access Centre (CCAC) staff look to the hierarchy of substitute decision makers (see page 95). A guardian of person is ranked highest on the list. If there is no guardian of person, an attorney for personal care could make the decision. If there is no attorney for personal care, staff at the CCAC continue down the list until an appropriate and willing substitute decision maker is found. If there are two or more persons in the decision making group and all of them want to act as substitute decision makers; for example, if three daughters were making the decision to place their mother, all three would have to be in agreement or the Public Guardian and Trustee may be called to make the decision in their place. Sometimes if there are two or more persons in the decision making group, family members (agree to) designate one member as the decision maker, in which case CCAC staff would communicate and work with the designated family member.

People who need care in a Long Term Care facility apply to have their name on the waiting list of at least one facility and no more than three. When an appropriate bed is available and their name is next on the waiting list, CCAC staff will call the person or their substitute decision maker and make a 'bed offer'. The person or their substitute decision maker has the opportunity to accept or refuse admission to the Long Term Care facility.

Admission may be refused because it is not the person's first choice facility or it may be that the person's health has improved and they hope to manage at home a little while longer. Since May 2002, CCAC staff are required to remove a person from all waiting lists if the person refuses an available bed in a home of their choice. The person is placed on a refusal list and unless their circumstances or condition worsens they cannot go back on a waiting list for a period of 24 weeks.

Admission to a Long Term Care facility is a difficult and emotional experience for most people and their families. If you do not have a Power of Attorney for Personal Care and if you suddenly became incapable, who does the *Health Care Consent Act* designate as your substitute decision maker? Is this the person or persons whom you would want making decisions on your behalf? If your answer is 'no', you need to consider giving a Power of Attorney for Personal Care to someone whom you could trust to make an admission decision for you.

Personal Assistance Services

Determining mental capacity and making decisions about personal assistance services

The *Health Care Consent Act* (Part IV, Personal Assistance Services) provides a process for making decisions on behalf of incapable residents of Long Term Care facilities. A personal assistance service means assistance with or supervision of hygiene, washing, dressing, grooming, eating drinking, elimination, ambulation, positioning, or any other routine activity of living. Long Term Care facilities have what is called a plan of care for each resident. The plan addresses the personal assistance needs of each resident, as well as any treatment and social needs.

People usually recognize their needs and accept help with activities such as dressing, eating, and ambulation. If the resident of a Long Term Care facility is found by an evaluator to be incapable with respect to a personal assistance service, a decision concerning the service may be made on the resident's behalf by his or her substitute decision maker (*Health Care Consent Act* (section 57)).

A substitute decision maker who makes a decision concerning a personal assistance service on behalf of an incapable resident shall do so in accordance with any wishes that the resident expressed while still capable. Or, if it is impossible to comply with the wish, the substitute could apply to the Consent and Capacity Board and ask for permission to depart from previous wishes. If the substitute decision maker doesn't know of any applicable wishes, the substitute decision maker shall make the decision in the resident's best interests.

As we end this chapter, **Important Things to Remember are:**

- The *Health Care Consent Act* protects your decision making rights related to treatment, admission to a Long Term Care facility, and personal assistance services in a Long Term Care facility.

- Any health practitioner (as defined in the Act) must obtain a valid consent from you or your substitute decision maker for any treatment that they are proposing before they administer the treatment.

- The health practitioner who proposes a treatment must determine whether the person is capable of giving or refusing consent.

- The health practitioner, in accordance with the health practitioner's College guidelines, must inform the person of his or her right to make application to the Consent and Capacity Board for a review of a finding of incapacity.

- For admission to a Long Term Care facility, an evaluator determines whether the person is capable of giving or refusing consent for admission. A person can only be admitted to a Long Term Care facility without consent in the case of an emergency.

- For personal assistance services in a Long Term Care facility, an evaluator determines whether the person is capable with respect to the personal assistance service.

11 Personal Care Decision Making Under the Substitute Decisions Act

The *Substitute Decisions Act* is the law that gives you the right to appoint an attorney for personal care. Both the *Substitute Decisions Act* and the *Health Care Consent Act* provide information about determining mental capacity and decision making processes for personal care decisions.

In this chapter …

- **when a person is mentally incapable of making personal care decisions**

- **assessment of mental capacity to make personal care decisions under the *Substitute Decisions Act***

    - **formal assessment**

    - **informal assessment when there is an attorney for personal care**

    - **informal assessment when there is no attorney for personal care**

- **who makes personal care decisions for an incapable person**

    - **guardian of the person**

    - **attorney for personal care**

The appointment of an attorney for personal care comes under the *Substitute Decisions Act*. The definition of incapacity to make a personal care decision and decision making rules that an attorney for personal care must follow come under both the *Substitute Decisions Act* and the *Health Care Consent Act*. Decision making under the *Health Care Consent Act* was discussed in the last chapter. This chapter will focus on other personal care decisions that come under the *Substitute Decisions Act*.

When is a person incapable of making personal care decisions?

The *Substitute Decisions Act* (section 45) tells us that a person is incapable of personal care if that person is not able to understand information that is relevant to making a decision concerning his or her own health care, nutrition, shelter, clothing, hygiene, or safety, or is not able to appreciate the reasonably foreseeable consequences of a decision or lack of decision. Health care in this definition does not include the three health care decisions (treatment, admission to a Long Term Care facility and personal assistance services) that come under the *Health Care Consent Act*.

> **A Power of Attorney for Personal Care only becomes effective when the grantor becomes incapable of making their own personal care decisions.**

Assessment of mental capacity to make personal care decisions under the *Substitute Decisions Act*

Formal assessment

Under the *Substitute Decisions Act* the terms capacity assessor and capacity assessment refer to a specific type of assessment which is conducted for specific purposes. Information about this process of assessment is found in Chapter 6. There are many other types of formal assessment which are conducted by doctors, psychologists, social workers and other professionals who have expertise assessing capacity. Assessments make use of a variety of tools that evaluate mood; perception; orientation to time, place, and person; memory and social judgement. The purpose of this section, however, is to focus on capacity assessment and decision making that pertains to personal care and the *Substitute Decisions Act*.

When is a formal capacity assessment for personal care required?

The use of formal capacity assessment in relation to personal care is limited to the following situations:

- the grantor of a power of attorney for personal care may want their incapacity to be confirmed before their attorney acts on their behalf. The grantor may specify that this is to be done by a capacity assessor. However, formal assessment of capacity is not a requirement of the law. The grantor also has the option of choosing an informal type of assessment, stating how and by whom capacity should be confirmed.

- the grantor of a power of attorney for personal care may want their incapacity to be confirmed before their attorney acts on their behalf but the document doesn't specify the method of capacity assessment. In this case, the attorney is only authorized to act when they receive notice from a capacity assessor that the grantor has been assessed and found to be incapable of personal care

- formal assessment by a capacity assessor is required in relation to the special provisions of section 50 of the *Substitute Decisions Act* (See Chapter 15.)

- in some cases, to arrange for or terminate a court-ordered guardianship of person

If the grantor's incapacity for personal care is confirmed by a capacity assessor and the grantor disagrees, the power of attorney could be revoked if the grantor still has the capacity to do so. There is no provision for appeal to the Consent and Capacity Board in this situation.

When is formal capacity assessment for personal care not required?

- before preparing a Power of Attorney for Personal Care, unless it includes the special provisions of section 50 of the *Substitute Decisions Act*

- if there is a power of attorney in place that does not require a formal capacity assessment to become effective

- when a substitute decision maker is authorized to make a personal care decision under the *Health Care Consent Act*

There is no provision for formal capacity assessment by a capacity assessor for decisions that come under the *Health Care Consent Act*. This Act provides for any required assessments to be done by either a health practitioner or an evaluator.

Emily Curtis is a 90 year old woman with dementia. She had given a Power of Attorney for Personal Care to her daughter, Pam, two years ago. Her husband Ralph, who is 92 years old, suffers from arthritis, but is mentally alert.

A year ago, Pam felt that her mother needed more care and she talked to her parents about going to live in a Long Term Care facility. Her parents agreed to go ahead with this plan. Because **admission** to a Long Term Care facility is a decision to which the *Health Care Consent Act* applies, Pam's parents were assessed by a nurse from a community nursing agency. Acting as an evaluator under the *Health Care Consent Act,* the nurse determined that Emily was incapable of making the decision to be admitted to a Long Term Care facility. Therefore, Pam, as Emily's attorney for personal care would need to make the decision for her. Ralph, on the other hand, was assessed as being mentally capable and could make his own decision to accept or refuse a bed when the time came.

Two weeks ago, the Placement Coordination Services coordinator called Pam and offered a bed for Emily at Parkway Lodge. Pam accepted on Emily's behalf and Emily was admitted.

Overcome by loneliness, Ralph arrived at Parkway Lodge yesterday wanting to take his wife home. Due to her dementia, Emily was willing to follow his lead. The Administrator at Parkway Lodge called on Pam as Emily's attorney for personal care to do something. Because **discharge** from a Long Term Care facility is a shelter decision that comes under the *Substitute Decisions Act*, Pam, as the attorney for personal care was able to assess her mother's capacity to make the decision. Based on discussions she had with her mother in the past and on what she believed to be in Emily's best interest, Pam decided that Emily needed to stay at Parkway. If Emily had not made Pam her attorney, Ralph would have taken his wife home. She would have lost her bed at the Long Term Care facility and Ralph's inability to care for her at home would have created a crisis for both of them.

In this situation Emily may have anticipated the difficulty her husband would have with the changes they were facing in the future and, therefore, made Pam her attorney for personal care. Because there were no instructions in the Power of Attorney for Personal Care about how or by whom capacity was to be determined, Pam was able to assess her mother's incapacity to make a discharge decision and act on her mother's behalf without delay.

Informal assessment of capacity when there is an attorney for personal care

An attorney for personal care can decide whether the grantor is incapable of making personal care decisions to which the *Substitute Decisions Act* (section 49 (1)(b)) applies. This happens when:

- the personal care decision has to do with safety, nutrition, clothing, shelter, hygiene and health decisions not covered by the *Health Care Consent Act*

- the attorney's authority has not been restricted to certain decisions. For example, the grantor has not said that the attorney can only make decisions about shelter and safety.

- any conditions in the Power of Attorney for Personal Care have been met

If the Power of Attorney for Personal Care contains instructions about how and by whom the grantor's capacity is to be determined, then these must be followed before the attorney can act. Care is needed so that instructions of this nature don't cause undue delay in the ability of the attorney to act on behalf of the grantor. Time can be a more important factor in making a personal care decision than it is in making a property decision.

Informal assessment of capacity when there is no attorney for personal care

As with the management of property, it is usually a person's network of social contacts who question and identify that someone is having difficulty managing their personal care. A person who is having difficulty with their personal care may take advice and act on the direction of another person. In this way, personal care needs may be met by informal supports including family and friends or by formal supports including community services. As long as the person is willing to follow directions and/or accept help from someone else a crisis may be averted. For example, someone might help a friend by doing their grocery shopping, or family may arrange for meals to be prepared if a person is not eating properly. Unfortunately, informal support is not always available or reliable. Community support services may be arranged but may be inadequate. Without an attorney for personal care, there may be no one to ensure that a person is eating or is being looked after. If there is no attorney for personal care, it is possible that some of a person's personal care needs will not be met and this could lead to suffering on their part.

There are examples of people who live in poor conditions where they refuse to accept the advice or help of others. They may be at risk of bodily harm and yet no one seems to be able to do anything. Even though the person may be incapable with respect to personal care, he or she may still be able to appoint an attorney for personal care in a Power of Attorney for Personal Care and this should always be investigated. Unfortunately, if someone is already refusing to accept advice or help, the appointment of an attorney may not make much difference.

Who makes personal care decisions for an incapable person?

Guardian of the person

A court-appointed guardian of the person is the highest ranking decision maker for a person who is incapable of personal care. If a person is incapable, has not appointed an attorney for personal care and requires personal care decisions to be made, someone may have to apply to the court to be appointed the incapable person's Guardian of Person. A formal capacity assessment may be required when an application for guardian of the person has been made. In situations where other types of formal assessments that are relevant to the application have already been done by an appropriate professional, such as a doctor, or a psychologist, the court may find this assessment information adequate and may not require a formal assessment by a capacity assessor under the *Substitute Decisions Act*.

Anyone may apply to a court to have a guardian of the person appointed for someone who is incapable of personal care and needs decisions to be made on their behalf (*Substitute Decisions Act* (Section 55 (1)). The decision making authority which a guardian of the person is given is stipulated in a court order. Once guardianship has been granted, it can only be terminated by a further judicial order. Guardianships may be full or partial, depending upon the capacity of the person to make decisions and upon the needs which they have.

The Public Guardian and Trustee may act as a guardian of property and/or a guardian of person, but this only occurs when no other suitable person, who is willing and able to act, has been found. You will recall that the formal assessment of a person's capacity and a finding of incapacity to manage property can result in statutory guardianship involving the Public Guardian and Trustee. There is no statutory guardianship for personal care. The *Substitute Decisions Act* does, however, make provision for the Public Guardian and Trustee to investigate a situation if serious adverse effects are suspected or have been identified.

> **Serious adverse effects related to personal care include serious illness, or deprivation of liberty or personal security.**

The *Substitute Decisions Act* requires the Public Guardian and Trustee to investigate any allegation that a person is incapable of personal care and that serious adverse effects are occurring or may occur as a result. Anyone can call the Public Guardian and Trustee to report such a case, but there must be clear evidence of serious adverse effects before an investigation will be made. The Public Guardian and Trustee does not do a formal assessment of mental capacity when informed about a person who is alleged to be in danger, but if, as a result of their investigation, the Public Guardian and Trustee has reasonable grounds to believe that a person is incapable of personal care and that the prompt appointment of a temporary guardian of the person is required to prevent serious adverse effects, the Public Guardian and Trustee can apply to the court for an order appointing him or her as the incapable person's temporary guardian of the person. The appointment is valid for a period fixed by the court that does not exceed ninety days.

> **Only a court-appointed guardian can make personal care decisions for someone who is mentally incapable and doesn't have an attorney for personal care. (Except where provisions of the *Mental Health Act* apply.)**

Court-appointed guardianship of the person occurs infrequently and should be viewed as a last resort where other measures do not adequately address the needs and best interests of an incapable person. It is beyond the scope of this book to discuss applications for guardianship. For more information the reader should refer to the *Substitute Decisions Act* (sections 55-68 and Part III) or call the office of the Public Guardian and Trustee.

Attorney for personal care

As discussed earlier, a formal capacity assessment may be required under the *Substitute Decisions Act* to activate a Power of Attorney for Personal Care. The power of attorney may be conditional on a finding of incapacity. Once the condition has been met, the attorney for personal care has the authority to act on behalf of the grantor.

A Power of Attorney for Personal Care may require an informal finding of incapacity before the attorney can act. When any such condition has been met, it is the attorney who has the authority to assess the grantor's capacity to make personal care decisions that come under the *Substitute Decision's Act* and to act on behalf of the grantor.

If there is a Power of Attorney for Personal Care that does not have conditions or restrictions, the attorney has the authority to determine whether the grantor is incapable of a personal care decision under the *Substitute Decisions Act* and has the authority to make personal care decisions for the grantor.

The *Health Care Consent Act* provides a list of substitute decision makers if a person doesn't have a guardian of personal care and has not appointed an attorney for personal care. The *Substitute Decisions Act* does not provide a list of substitute decision makers for personal care decisions under this Act. A person who chooses not to appoint an attorney for personal care may create a risk for him or herself. The ways to help someone in this position are limited and someone may have to apply to the court to be appointed the person's guardian.

As we end this chapter, **Important Things to Remember are:**

- **A person is considered to be incapable of personal care when**

    o **they don't understand information that is relevant to making decisions about health care, nutrition, clothing, shelter, hygiene, or safety**

    o **they don't appreciate the reasonably, foreseeable consequences of making the decision or not making the decision**

- **A Power of Attorney for Personal Care is effective when the grantor is incapable of making personal care decisions.**

- **Assessment of mental capacity to make personal care decisions under the *Health Care Consent Act* is done by a health practitioner or an evaluator. (See Chapter 10.)**

- **The grantor can include instructions in the Power of Attorney for Personal Care about how and by whom incapacity is to be determined. Assessment of mental capacity to make personal care decisions under the *Substitute Decisions Act* can be made by the attorney if the grantor makes no other provision regarding assessment.**

12 Your Decision to Make a Power of Attorney for Personal Care

One of the best reasons to appoint an attorney in a Power of Attorney for Personal Care is to ensure that someone who knows your beliefs, values and wishes can make personal care decisions for you if you ever become mentally incapable.

In this chapter ...

- reasons for appointing an attorney for personal care

  - you want a decision maker other than the one designated by law

  - mental incapacity is anticipated

  - family disagreement is anticipated

  - personal assistance services may be required in a private home setting

- preparation of a power of attorney for personal care

  - conditions and restrictions

  - wishes and instructions

  - responsibilities of the grantor

Most of us should have a Continuing Power of Attorney for Property. The question of whether you should have a Power of Attorney for Personal Care is something that only you can answer. Before appointing an attorney for personal care you need to carefully consider all of the following factors that work together to make unique your life situation and your need for an attorney for personal care.

- your values and beliefs related to personal care
- family relationships
- your present and future care needs
- your place of residence.

People may feel that the provisions for substitute decision making in the *Health Care Consent Act* adequately cover their personal care decision making needs. They have reviewed the list of substitute decision makers and are satisfied that the person who would be asked to act as their substitute is the person they would select. They feel there is no need to appoint an attorney for personal care. There are some situations, however, in which a Power of Attorney for Personal Care can be of benefit and should be encouraged.

Reasons for appointing an attorney for personal care

When you want a decision maker other than the one designated by law

Having reviewed the list of substitute decision makers in the *Health Care Consent Act* (reviewed in chapter 10 of this book), you may not want the person with the highest ranking to make personal care decisions on your behalf. In case the highest ranking substitute decision maker is unwilling or unable to act, you should also consider whether you would want those who are ranked second or third to act on your behalf. If you have any concerns about who might be called upon to make personal care decisions for you, an attorney for personal care should be appointed.

Kirsten Hart is a 24 year old single woman whose parents divorced when she was eighteen. Kirsten never got along well with her mother and although they live in the same city they have little contact. Kirsten gets along well with her father but last year he remarried and moved to another city. After attending a community information meeting about powers of attorney Kirsten realizes that without an attorney for personal care the law designates both her mother and father to make decisions for her. Kirsten used the power of attorney kit from the Public Guardian and Trustee's office to appoint her father and her friend Sara as her attorneys for personal care with authority to act jointly and severally.

When family disagreement is anticipated

In situations where family disagreement can be anticipated, an attorney for personal care should be appointed. Chronic or terminal illness, dementia or mental health problems can raise questions that people have never before considered. Disagreements about medical treatment or end of life care may be based on the moral, ethical, or spiritual beliefs of individual family members. By appointing an attorney for personal care, you ensure that someone you trust will follow your specific wishes and instructions.

When mental incapacity is anticipated

If there are medical conditions where mental incapacity is anticipated you should appoint an attorney for personal care. These medical conditions might include different mental disorders or degenerative neurological conditions such as Parkinsons Disease or Multiple Sclerosis. The appointment of an attorney for personal care gives you the opportunity to discuss your wishes and instructions with others and to plan for substitute decision making.

When personal assistance services may be required in a private home setting

The provision of personal assistance services to an incapable person who lives in a Long Term Care facility is governed by the *Health Care Consent Act*. It is possible, however, for some incapable people to be cared for at home or in a place other than a Long Term Care facility. Decisions about nutrition, clothing, shelter, safety, and hygiene may be required in these settings. If an attorney for personal care has not been appointed and decisions not covered by the *Health Care Consent Act* are required, a family member may be faced with the complexity and cost of having to make application to become a court-appointed guardian of the person.

Preparation of a power of attorney for personal care

This section will inform you about some of the issues that deserve your consideration and thought when you are going to make a Power of Attorney for Personal Care.

Conditions and Restrictions

A condition is a requirement that must be met before the attorney can act. By providing a third party assessor, the *Health Care Consent Act* has a built in condition. A health practitioner or an evaluator, must always determine a person's mental capacity to make a particular treatment or admission decision before consent is requested from the person or their attorney. For non *Health Care Consent Act* decisions, the attorney has the authority to determine mental capacity and make a decision without the involvement of a third party.

Some grantors want a third party involved when a non *Health Care Consent Act* decision is going to be made and this can be achieved by including conditions such as, requiring the attorney to notify another family member when the attorney makes a decision or to consult with a friend or spiritual advisor.

If you have named more than one attorney, you may want to specify whose decision is to be followed if there is disagreement.

A restriction is an area in which the attorney is denied authority. When you make a Power of Attorney for Personal Care you need to decide whether you are giving your attorney authority over all areas of personal care or whether you want to limit their authority to certain categories. For example, the grantor could restrict the attorney's decision making to areas covered by the *Health Care Consent Act,* in which case the attorney would be restricted from making other personal care decisions such as nutrition, clothing, hygiene, etc. Think carefully about any restrictions that you impose because if you become incapable and your attorney doesn't have authority to decide for you, it may be necessary for the court to appoint a guardian.

Regardless of the authority that an attorney has, they can only make personal care decisions that the grantor is incapable of making for him or herself.

Many Powers of Attorney for Personal Care are written with no conditions, restrictions, or instructions. If you and your attorney trust one another implicitly, the transfer of decision making power can happen without disagreement or worry.

Wishes and Instructions

Instructions do not have to be written down in a Power of Attorney for Personal Care. When they are included, care should be used in writing instructions about future, theoretical situations. We are all born with a strong sense of survival and while we are enjoying good health, how well can any of us predict the decisions that we might make in a time of crisis? Unless a person is already living with a diagnosed illness or condition, it is difficult to know how he or she might react in an unforeseen situation.

Some forms for creating Powers of Attorney for Personal Care contain standard end of life clauses with specific instructions. Great care should be taken when using these standard clauses. You, as the grantor, must be clear about what the clause is saying and sure that you would want your attorney to act on a specific instruction such as this.

When instructions are written on extra pages of paper or in separate documents (such as Living Wills or Advance Health Care Directives) the grantor can easily make changes to these notes without having to revoke their Power of Attorney for Personal Care and execute a new one. It is a good idea to initial each page of any supplementary notes or forms and attach them to your power of attorney.

Caution: When using standard Advance Health Care Directive or Living Will forms, some may contain clauses that revoke any previous Power of Attorney for Personal Care. If you are using such a form as a supplement to your Power of Attorney for Personal Care, make sure that the form doesn't contain a clause that revokes your existing Power of Attorney for Personal Care and the appointment of your attorney.

Caution: A Living Will may name a decision maker, but unless the Living Will is also a Power of Attorney for Personal Care (that is, the document appoints an attorney and is properly signed and witnessed), the decision maker named in the Living Will will not have authority to make decisions for you unless the *Health Care Consent Act* designates the same decision maker.

Steven Silverstein and Jarod Thompson have lived together as a gay couple for the past twenty years. Ten years ago they prepared wills and powers of attorney for property to ensure that their assets would pass to one another on the death of the first partner and that they would have decision making authority over all of their property if one partner became incapable. Last year they prepared Living Wills on forms from a local book store. They appointed each other to make treatment decisions and recorded some instructions. The forms didn't provide a place for two witnesses to sign but they asked two of their friends to be witnesses. After Steven and Jarod signed their Living Wills they had their two friends sign below their signatures. By doing this they ensured that each form met the legal requirement to be a valid Power of Attorney for Personal Care even though it was called a Living Will.

Responsibilities of the grantor

The appointment of an attorney for personal care means that the grantor has the benefit of having selected the person of their choice to make personal care decisions if the grantor should ever become incapable.

In order to enhance the quality of decisions that an attorney for personal care might make on behalf of the grantor, the grantor has a responsibility to prepare the attorney to assume this role. If you have been close to someone for most of your life and share similar beliefs and values, that person will have a better chance of making decisions as you would rather than someone who has beliefs and values that are different from yours. There is always the possibility that your attorney may not have the instructions that they need for a particular situation and, in the absence of clear instruction, may not decide exactly as you would. Rather than instructions, or in addition to instructions, you might consider preparing a statement of values and beliefs that could be used to give your attorney guidance when making decisions. In the absence of instructions, someone who understands your beliefs and values will have a better sense of how you might decide in any given situation.

After the preparation of a Power of Attorney for Personal Care, the grantor has another important responsibility. The attorney needs to know how to access the original, signed power of attorney document. If mental incapacity is anticipated, people generally plan for this transfer of power. If incapacity is not anticipated and the Power of Attorney for Personal Care is made as insurance against some future medical emergency, your attorney needs to know where the document is and what it says. Remember, in the event of an emergency you won't be able to tell them. Some people have left their power of attorney documents with their lawyer for safekeeping along with their will. Some people store their documents in a safe place at home. Either practice is acceptable as long as your attorney knows where the document is and has the authority to access it. Valid documents are useless if the location or method of release is unknown.

As we end this chapter, **Important Things to Remember are:**

- **Appointing an attorney for personal care is important if you do not agree with the substitute decision maker that the law designates; you anticipate mental incapacity due to illness or disease; you anticipate family members of equal standing would disagree about decisions required on your behalf; or you are receiving personal care services at home or in a place other than a Long Term Care facility.**

- **If you write instructions in an Advance Directive or Living Will, instead of in the Power of Attorney for Personal Care, you can change those instructions in the future without making a new Power of Attorney for Personal Care.**

- **It is not possible to anticipate every situation where mental incapacity might occur or how we would react in a given situation, so the grantor has a responsibility to discuss their wishes and instructions with their attorney.**

Part IV

More About Making and Using Powers of Attorney

13 Some Practical Considerations

If you have decided that you need to prepare a power of attorney, you may have questions about how the document should be prepared. If someone has given you power of attorney, you may have questions about using the document.

In this chapter …

- power of attorney forms

- preparation of documents

- storage of documents

- making copies

- using powers of attorney

This chapter answers some of the questions you may have if you've decided to make a Continuing Power of Attorney for Property or a Power of Attorney for Personal Care.

Is there a special form that's needed to make a power of attorney?

No. The *Substitute Decisions Act* (sections 7 (7.1) and 46 (8)) states that the power of attorney need not be in any particular form. However, forms for both types of powers of attorney are available from the Public Guardian and Trustee's Office at no cost to you. These forms are similar in content to the forms that are used by most lawyers or paralegals. There is space on the form for you to appoint your attorney(s). There is a statement revoking any previous powers of attorney. The form also includes larger blank spaces where conditions, restrictions and/or instructions can be written or left blank. There is a place for the grantor and the two witnesses to sign at the end.

Regardless of the form you use, if your power of attorney document is not executed (signed) by yourself and two witnesses in accordance with the *Substitute Decisions Act*, it is not a valid power of attorney.

Advance Health Care Directive or Living Will forms are intended to provide you with a way of recording your wishes and instructions about personal care. Some Advance Health Care Directive and Living Will forms also contain statements in which you can appoint an attorney for personal care, which in effect makes the document into a Power of Attorney for Personal Care. There is nothing wrong with this, but you need to note the following:

- if you intend the Advance Health Care Directive or Living Will to be considered a valid Power of Attorney for Personal Care, the Directive or Living Will must appoint an attorney and be signed in accordance with the directions in the *Substitute Decisions Act*

- be clear about whether the Advance Health Care Directive or Living Will revokes previous Powers of Attorney for Personal Care and whether this is your intention

- if you want to appoint an attorney for property, it must be done in a separate, Continuing Power of Attorney for Property document

Can I prepare my own power of attorney documents or should I have a lawyer prepare the documents?

You can prepare your own powers of attorney. The forms that are produced by the Public Guardian and Trustee's Office come with a fairly comprehensive instruction guide. Unfortunately, there is very little other literature that is available to help you. Even if you intend to give your attorney full authority with no restrictions or conditions, you need to understand the implications of what you are doing and the choices that are available to you. It may be worth the cost to have a lawyer or other trained professional talk to you about your situation and prepare documents that reflect your particular needs. Also, if you work with a professional and you need to make a change to your power of attorney in the future, some professionals will make the revisions for a reduced fee.

If you purchase a kit or forms and prepare your own documents, you do so at your own risk because some kits contain incorrect information. By using a kit you've also missed the benefit of discussing your needs and receiving valuable information. If changes are needed you may be looking at further expense and, of course, if there's a problem with your documents, you could end up paying much more to have the problem sorted out in court.

What you pay to have a power of attorney prepared is not necessarily a reflection of the quality of work or information that you receive. It partly reflects the professional person's hourly rate. You may pay a lot and get a little. You may pay less and get a lot. Make sure you get your money's worth!

Where should I keep my powers of attorney once they are signed?

People often begin to think about storage of their powers of attorney after the documents have been prepared. Obviously, safety of the documents and access to them are primary considerations, but the time to think about storage is before you make a power of attorney, not after. It is a good idea to imagine different scenarios in which your power of attorney might be needed and to think about how your attorney would gain access to the document in order to act on your behalf. The following examples are meant to show the individual nature of this decision.

Ella Rybeck is a middle aged lady with two daughters who live about an hour from where she lives. Ella rents an apartment and has very few assets. Recently, she has appointed her two daughters as her attorneys, acting jointly and severally, in a Continuing Power of Attorney for Property and in a Power of Attorney for Personal Care. All of her important papers are kept in a safety deposit box at the bank. She wants to keep her powers of attorney there, but appreciates that if she became mentally incapable, her daughters would not have access to the documents. She discussed this with the girls and they agreed that the safety deposit box was the best place to keep the documents. So her daughters went to the bank with Ella and were given joint and several signing authority with her for the safety deposit box.

Bob and Rosemary Becker have been happily married for ten years. They have two young children and have just recently bought their first home. Wanting to have all their affairs in order, they have prepared wills and powers of attorney. They share similar beliefs and values and trust one another to make decisions for each other if anything ever happened. They have named each other as their attorney and have named Rosemary's father as an alternate attorney. They have a small fire proof safe at home and this is where they keep all their valuables and important papers. Rosemary's father has been informed of this and has a key to the safe.

The examples given above represent uncomplicated family situations. In cases where there is family conflict or poor relationships, or more than moderate wealth, the grantor might choose to store documents with the lawyer and have him or her involved with the release of the documents. Plans for storage of your powers of attorney should be discussed as part of the assessment of your needs. You should also think about how your attorney would access your other documents if you were mentally incapable and whether you want to include instructions about this in the power of attorney. This, in turn, can affect where and by whom your powers of attorney and other documents are stored.

> **Regardless of where you store your powers of attorney, your attorney must know where they are and how to access the original, signed documents.**

Should I make photocopies of my powers of attorney?

You may want to make photocopies of your powers of attorney for your reference and information and that of your attorney, particularly if the originals are being stored somewhere other than at your home. It is a good idea to give your attorney(s) a copy so that they know what you expect of them. They may have questions and it may prompt discussion with you about your values, beliefs, and wishes.

If you become incapable and your attorney needs to act on your behalf, your attorney will probably need to obtain certified copies of your powers of attorney. Each agency or institution that the attorney must deal with on your behalf will want to see the power of attorney document. A photocopy does not provide adequate proof for matters related to property management. A photocopy may be accepted for personal care decisions, but if there is any question or dispute over the attorney's appointment, a certified copy will be requested.

One of the power of attorney kits that you can buy comes with a separate wallet sized card which is a miniature duplicate of your power of attorney document. The idea is that by signing this card your attorney will be able to carry this original proof of their appointment with them without the bother of carrying bulky documents or of obtaining certified copies. Remember that a special form is not needed to make a power of attorney and even a small sized card can be a valid document if it contains the necessary information and is signed in accordance with the law. Always be careful that a duplicate card is exactly the same as your full sized document and that a card signed later doesn't revoke a previously signed document.

The practice of signing multiple copies of powers of attorney should be approached with caution. Your powers of attorney are very powerful documents so you want to ensure that there is controlled access to the documents. If you sign an extra copy for your lawyer to keep in case your substitute attorney needs to act, controlled access will be maintained through the lawyer.

Signing multiple copies, as a way of avoiding the need to obtain certified copies, is not recommended. There may be reason in the future for you to revoke your power of attorney and multiple signed copies could create real problems for you. The safest way of controlling and managing the work that your attorney will do on your behalf is to have them obtain certified copies when they begin to act on your behalf. Certified copies can be obtained for a small fee from any court house office and many lawyers.

If I appoint an attorney in a General Power of Attorney, do I still need a Continuing Power of Attorney for Property?

Since 1995, when the laws changed, a General Power of Attorney is usually only given when a mentally capable grantor requires an attorney to complete a particular transaction on the grantor's behalf or to act for a specified period of time on the grantor's behalf. A Continuing Power of Attorney for Property, on the other hand, usually gives the attorney authority over all areas and is made in consideration of future mental incapacity.

A General Power of Attorney is not a substitute for a Continuing Power of Attorney for Property. A Continuing Power of Attorney for Property (if there are no restrictions) gives your attorney full authority to do on your behalf whatever you can do (except make a will). Besides managing income and spending, this includes filing tax returns, some types of investing, making loans and real estate transactions.

What can an attorney for property expect when they begin to act on the grantor's behalf?

An attorney for property should ensure that the grantor has written down a summary of bank locations and account numbers; information about investments, safety deposit boxes, RRSP's and insurance policies; and information about any other assets and obligations.

When an attorney takes a certified copy of the Continuing Power of Attorney for Property to the bank, the bank will want to know whether the grantor is mentally capable or incapable. Banks are very protective of their customer's assets (which we can all appreciate), and because of this the bank manager may ask you for more information than is actually required. It's helpful to understand the difference between what the law requires and what the bank wants.

If an attorney is in possession of a valid Continuing Power of Attorney for Property document and has met the conditions for its use, the document itself is proof of the attorney's authority to act and of the nature of their authority.

The following situations describe the different ways that bank personnel may respond to an attorney with a Continuing Power of Attorney for Property when:

- the grantor is capable

    If the grantor is capable the bank will probably want some kind of communication from the grantor (verbal or written) to verify the specific nature of the authority that the grantor is giving to the attorney. For example, does the grantor intend the attorney to have full control of the grantor's finances or do they just want them to pay bills from a chequing account? They may ask the grantor to complete a General Power of Attorney form. This is not necessary and it could revoke a valid Continuing Power of Attorney for Property unless there is provision in it for multiple powers of attorney. Be very careful.

- the grantor is incapable and use of the power of attorney is not contingent on any conditions

    In this case, the Continuing Power of Attorney for Property document is proof of the attorney's authority. Although no further information is required for the attorney to act, you may find that the bank requests more information before they are willing to work with the attorney. You might suggest that they check with their head office or call the grantor's lawyer to get things going.

- The grantor is incapable and the release of the Continuing Power of Attorney for Property is contingent on assessment by a third party, such as a doctor or a lawyer. Documentation from the third party should be attached to the power of attorney and should be adequate for the bank to recognize the attorney's power.

If the use of a power of attorney for property is anticipated, it would be wise to visit the bank. Getting to know the bank manager and having them assist with planning can help things to go more smoothly when the attorney needs to act.

What can an attorney for personal care expect when they begin to act on the grantor's behalf?

A Power of Attorney for Personal Care is a relatively new and different type of power of attorney. An attorney for personal care will primarily deal with health care professionals and social service agencies. One certified copy of the document may be adequate. The health professional or agency may or may not want to make a photocopy.

Because the laws are relatively new, many health professionals remain uncertain about the requirements and procedures related to a Power of Attorney for Personal Care. If an attorney for personal care is giving consent to a proposed treatment, things usually go smoothly. If the attorney is refusing to consent to treatment or personal care on an incapable person's behalf, there may be some difficulty. It can be intimidating to disagree with any professional person, but an attorney is obligated to follow the wishes and instructions of the grantor. It is important for the attorney to understand their rights and the health care professional's duty to the attorney and the grantor.

As we end this chapter, **Important Things to Remember are:**

- **Powers of attorney do not need to be in any particular form.**

- **You can prepare your own powers of attorney, but to be valid they must be executed in accordance with the *Substitute Decisions Act*. The price you pay to have documents prepared by a lawyer or other trained professional may be worth it in terms of information and compliance with the law.**

- **Where you decide to store your documents requires some thoughtful consideration. Make sure your attorney knows where the documents are and how to access them.**

- **A General Power of Attorney is not a substitute for a Continuing Power of Attorney for Property and is not required in addition to a Continuing Power of Attorney for Property.**

- **Each agency or institution with which an attorney has to deal will require proof of the attorney's authority, so an attorney will probably have to obtain certified copies of the documents after they begin to act.**

14 Consent and Capacity Board

The law provides for the Consent and Capacity Board to hear applications that are brought to the Board for certain matters under the *Health Care Consent Act,* the *Mental Health Act*, the *Substitute Decisions Act*, and the *Long Term Care Act.*

In this chapter ...

- **Consent and Capacity Board powers**

- **matters that can be brought to the Consent and Capacity Board**

- **procedures at a hearing**

Consent and capacity laws in Ontario have created systems in which every effort has been made to protect the decision making rights of individuals. For approximately thirty years there have been Boards of various names whose responsibility it was to hear matters related to mental incapacity under the *Mental Health Act.* The jurisdiction of these Boards was limited to psychiatric facilities. In 1995, with the introduction of the *Substitute Decisions Act* and the *Consent to Treatment Act* (later replaced by the *Health Care Consent Act),* the Board at that time was renamed the Consent and Capacity Review Board. In addition to previous responsibilities, the Consent and Capacity Review Board was given the power to review capacity and related matters. A year later, in March 1996, with the revision of the new laws, the Board was renamed again, and is now known as the Consent and Capacity Board. Responsibilities of the Consent and Capacity Board were further expanded to include duties related to capacity to give consent for admission to a Long Term Care facility and personal assistance services in a Long Term Care facility.

The *Health Care Consent Act* (Part V) is the law which establishes the Consent and Capacity Board. The Consent and Capacity Board is a tribunal created by the provincial government. It is not a court and it only has powers which the law gives to it. The Consent and Capacity Board tries to resolve issues in an informal way and it acts independently of health care institutions, government agencies, doctors and other health professionals.

Matters that can be brought to the Consent and Capacity Board

Health Care Consent Act

- review of a finding that a person is not capable of making decisions with respect to

  - treatment (section 32(1))
  - admission to a Long Term Care facility (section 50 (1))
  - personal assistance services in a Long Term Care facility (section 65(1))

- application for appointment of a representative to make decisions for an incapable person regarding treatment, admission to a Long Term Care facility or personal assistance services in a Long Term Care facility

- application to amend or terminate the appointment of a representative

- review of a decision to admit an incapable person to a hospital or psychiatric facility, Nursing Home or Home for the Aged for the purpose of treatment

- application from a substitute decision maker for directions concerning wishes

- consideration of a request from a substitute decision maker for authority to depart from the prior wishes of a person made while they were capable

Note: A health practitioner or substitute decision maker can only apply for permission to consent to a treatment or service if the grantor's wishes were to refuse the treatment or service. The health practitioner or substitute decision maker cannot apply for permission to refuse, if the grantor's wishes were to have the treatment or service.

- review of a substitute decision maker's compliance with the rules for substitute decision making

Mental Health Act

- review of involuntary status

An involuntary patient is someone who is detained at a psychiatric facility because there is evidence that the patient is suffering from a mental disorder and as a result the patient may cause bodily harm to him or herself or others.

An involuntary patient, or any person on his or her behalf, may apply to the Consent and Capacity Board for a review of the patient's status. Application may be made when a Certificate of Involuntary Admission (Form 3) or a Certificate of Renewal (Form 4) comes into force (section 39(2)). As well, application may be made at any time by the Minister, Deputy Minister, or the officer in charge regarding any involuntary patient (section 39(3)). (A patient detained for a 72 hour assessment under an Application for Psychiatric Assessment (Form 1) is not entitled to a review, but they must be given an explanation of the detention and advised of their right to contact a lawyer.)

- review of a Community Treatment Order

- review as to whether a young person (aged 12 to 15 years) requires observation, care and treatment in a psychiatric facility

- review of a finding of incapacity to manage property

- review of competency to access or allow others to access the patient's clinical record

- consideration of the appointment of a representative for the purpose of disclosure or access to records

- consideration of a request from a psychiatric facility to withhold access to a clinical record

Substitute Decisions Act

- review of statutory guardianship of property

Long Term Care Act

- consideration of a request to withhold access to a clinical record

Hearing Procedures

The road we travel from the point where we are able to make our own decisions to the point where someone else makes decisions for us is not always smooth. The laws under which matters can be brought to the Consent and Capacity Board cover different types of decisions and provide a method of resolution where there is disagreement.

The Consent and Capacity Board has no power to initiate a hearing on its own and can only conduct a hearing if requested to do so. Anyone can apply for a hearing, including the person who is the object of the hearing. Board members are psychiatrists, lawyers, and members of the general public, and depending on the type of application, the Board may sit with one, three, or five members. A hearing is usually scheduled within a week after the Board receives the application and it is usually held in the home or facility where the person who is the subject of the hearing resides, or at another place convenient to the parties. Each party to the hearing may invite anyone they want to attend. Each party may have a lawyer, call witnesses and bring documents. Each party and the Board members may ask questions of each witness. Hearings are recorded (usually on videotape) in case a transcript is required. After the hearing, the Board will meet in private to make its decision and will give its decision to the parties within one day. Written reasons for the decision will be given if any of the parties to the hearing request them within thirty days of the hearing.

The Consent and Capacity Board is publicly funded and there is no charge to the participants for the services of the Board. Except, if parties retain a lawyer, in which case, the lawyer's fees are the party's own. Application forms are available from health or residential facilities. Or, forms and information sheets can be obtained by calling the Consent and Capacity Board office at 1-800-461-2036.

Sometimes the determination of capacity is not straight forward and this is why the law provides for an application to the Board to review the findings of an assessor. Subsequently, any decision of the Consent and Capacity Board can be appealed to the Ontario Superior Court of Justice. In the few cases that have come before the courts, every effort has been made to uphold the rights of mentally capable individuals to make their own decisions.

As we end this chapter, **Important Things to Remember are:**

- **The Consent and Capacity Board is a non-partisan tribunal established by the** *Health Care Consent Act* **(Part V).**

- **The Consent and Capacity Board hears applications that are brought to it under the** *Health Care Consent Act*, **the** *Mental Health Act*, **the** *Substitute Decisions Act* **and the** *Long Term Care Act*.

- **Anyone can make application to the Consent and Capacity Board to have the Board review matters that are under its jurisdiction.**

15 Exceptional Circumstances

Procedures are usually written to address what is expected to happen under normal circumstances, but people and their life situations are not always predictable. Substitute decision making laws make some provisions for unusual and exceptional circumstances.

In this chapter ...

- **dealing with objections**

  - **a special provision in the *Substitute Decisions Act* for the use of reasonable force**

  - **verbal objection**

  - **physical resistance**

- **emergency treatment**

Dealing with Objections

The dictionary defines "objection" as an expression of disapproval. Making an application for review by the Consent and Capacity Board is one way people are able to object or express their disapproval related to findings of mental incapacity. Sometimes people express their objection to decisions made on their behalf in other ways. Disapproval can also be expressed by objecting verbally or by physically resisting a required action.

Special provision to use reasonable force

The law works toward ensuring that a decision maker of your choice will have the authority to make decisions if and when you are mentally incapable and require the decision maker's help. It is not uncommon for an incapable person to verbally object to decisions being made by the decision maker and in some cases, to even exhibit aggressive or other difficult behaviours. If behavioral problems are to be anticipated, there is a special provision in the *Substitute Decisions Act* that makes it possible for the grantor to give their attorney for personal care more powerful authority.

The *Substitute Decisions Act* (section 50) describes special provisions that authorize an attorney to use force "that is reasonable and necessary" with respect to the assessment and/or treatment of the grantor. If the grantor includes this special provision, they waive their right to apply to the Consent and Capacity Board for a review of a finding of incapacity. The provision is sometimes referred to as a Ulysses contract. The classical hero, Ulysses, knew that he would be unable to resist the seductive singing of the sirens and that following their songs would lead to the destruction of his ship and crew. He plugged the men's ears with wax and ordered them to tie him to the mast. They were to disregard his orders when he was affected by the sirens' call.

The waiving of one's right of appeal is a drastic step and can only be done if the grantor is capable of understanding the implications of this choice. Therefore, if a grantor wishes to include this provision in their Power of Attorney for Personal Care, the procedure requires formal assessment by a capacity assessor to confirm the grantor's mental capacity to understand and include the provision. The grantor must sign a special form, provided by the capacity assessor, in which the grantor indicates an understanding of the effect of the provision and of the waiving of their right to apply to the Consent and Capacity Board. If the grantor subsequently changes his or her mind and wishes to revoke the provision and/or the Power of Attorney for Personal Care, a similar process of capacity assessment is again required. Formal assessment by an assessor and special signed statements by the grantor and the assessor are required in order to confirm the grantor's capacity to revoke the document.

This provision appears to be an extreme measure, but if the grantor has a disease in which aggression or unmanageable behaviour is anticipated, the grantor should be made aware of the provision and given the opportunity to discuss its implications with those who will be expected to act on the grantor's behalf. It would also be wise for the grantor to seek medical and/or legal advice if they are considering the use of this provision.

Verbal Objection

Although the law states that a person's capable wishes must be followed, it also recognizes that there may be circumstances that make it difficult for the attorney or substitute decision maker to follow those wishes (*Health Care Consent Act* (section 21(1)). Stressful situations and confrontation can result when a person, who has been assessed as incapable, is verbally objecting to a health care decision. A screaming child who is resisting an immunization needle can leave their mother feeling emotionally drained. A care giver who must place a spouse in a nursing home because the care giver's own health is in jeopardy can feel tremendous loss and guilt. Usually with support and encouragement, the incapable person will follow the direction which is given, even though he or she may continue to express dislike and/or disapproval. The incapable person's verbal objection does not necessarily take precedence over the decision that is required. This is often the case when a person has to move to a nursing home or retirement home because of increasing care needs.

> **The verbal objection of an incapable person should not be regarded as refusal to give consent because an incapable person cannot give consent.**

Decision making can also strain family relationships when an incapable person objects to a decision. Sometimes the attorney or substitute decision maker can find him or herself caught between the incapable person and other family members who have their own opinions on what should be done. Ultimately, the decision must always be made in the best interest of the incapable person (*Health Care Consent Act* (section 21(2)).

Unfortunately, many of us at some point in our lives may have to face a situation where all of the choices seem to be unsatisfactory. If you are making personal care decisions for an incapable person and there is any kind of disagreement or conflict, the following suggestions may help:

- staff of hospitals or agencies that are helping the incapable person should be able to counsel family members individually or as a group

Having information about each option and what it means can help family members to focus on the decision and to understand why a particular decision has to be made, rather than criticizing the person who has to make it.

- sometimes family members try to avoid confrontation with the incapable person by not telling them what is happening

No matter how difficult, the incapable person always has a right to be informed. (Think of how you would want to be treated.) Again, professional help may be needed to understand feelings of anger, guilt or frustration and to encourage communication among family members.

- family discussion and advance planning is another way to prepare for future decision making

When someone has a mental health problem, a chronic illness, or a deteriorating condition, there are often opportunities while the person is still capable to discuss what the person's wishes are. Preparation of powers of attorney and a health directive can reduce the stress of decision making and family conflict when the person becomes incapable or reaches a point of crisis.

Physical Resistance

Objection is most difficult to manage when an incapable person physically resists compliance with decisions made by their substitute decision maker.

The *Health Care Consent Act* (section 24) limits the actions that can be taken if the incapable person has a mental health problem. According to the Act an incapable person can be admitted to a hospital or psychiatric facility for treatment with the consent of their substitute decision maker, so long as the incapable person is not objecting to the admission. If an incapable person is 16 years or older and objects to being admitted to a psychiatric facility for treatment of a mental disorder, consent can only be given by

- a guardian of the person (if the guardian has the authority to consent to the admission), or

- an attorney for personal care if the Power of Attorney for Personal Care contains the special provision (*Substitute Decisions Act*, section 50) to use reasonable force

The Ontario *Mental Health Act* defines mental disorder as, "any disease or disability of the mind". This is a very broad definition and is not limited to specific psychiatric diagnoses. A mental disorder usually causes impairment of a person's intellectual functioning, emotions, behaviour, perception of reality and/or the ability to engage in wilful, voluntary courses of action. Physical illness such as infection and dehydration; or diseases such as Parkinsons Disease, Multiple Sclerosis, and end stage renal disease, can also result in mental disorder.

George Williams is an 80 year old man who had been living in the Blackmore Boarding Home in the downtown area for almost five years. His only relative is a niece who visits him at Christmas. The owner of the home was concerned about George because recently he had been losing weight and staying in his room more than usual. When George failed to pay his rent, the owner of the home got in touch with his niece, Susan Long. When Susan arrived to visit, it was obvious to her that George was not well. Despite her efforts, she could not convince him to see a doctor. Susan contacted the local Health Unit and a public health nurse agreed to visit. By now George was laying on his bed all day, refusing food, incontinent, and refusing any kind of assistance with his personal care. Without his consent and cooperation, it was impossible to assess his condition, or to provide treatment and care. What could be done? How could Susan get him the help that was so badly needed?

In this case, if George had not had family, the Public Guardian and Trustee could have been called to investigate serious adverse effects. Because George had a niece who was willing to help him, other action was necessary. Susan could have applied to be George's court-appointed guardian of person, but the time required to do this (not to mention the expense) was prohibitive. The *Mental Health Act* provided Susan with another course of action.

Section 15: By order of a physician (Form 1)

If the following three requirements are met, any physician in Ontario may order a person to be taken into custody and brought to a psychiatric facility for up to 72 hours for an assessment:

- the physician has examined the person within the last seven days

- the physician has reasonable cause to believe the person fits one of the following criteria:

    ○ has threatened/is threatening to cause bodily harm to him or herself

    ○ has attempted/is attempting to cause bodily harm to him or herself

    ○ has behaved/is behaving violently towards others

    ○ has caused or is causing another person to fear bodily harm from him or her

- ○ has shown or is showing a lack of competence to care for him or herself

- the physician is of the opinion that the person apparently has a mental disorder of a nature or quality that will likely result in one or more of the following:

  - ○ serious bodily harm to the person

  - ○ serious bodily harm to another person

  - ○ imminent and serious physical impairment

George Williams did not have a family doctor and had refused to let his niece take him to see any doctor; therefore, a Form 1 could not be used to help him. One other course of action was available to Susan.

Section 16: By order of a justice of the peace (Form 2)

If the following two requirements are met, a justice of the peace may order a person to be taken into custody and brought before a physician for a Section 15 examination:

- Information on oath is brought before the justice, stating that the person fits any one of the following criteria:

  - ○ has threatened/is threatening to cause bodily harm to him or herself

  - ○ has attempted/is attempting to cause bodily harm to him or herself

  - ○ has behaved/is behaving violently towards other

  - ○ has caused or is causing another person to fear bodily harm

  - ○ has shown or is showing lack of competence to care for him or herself

- based on the information before him or her, the justice has reason to believe that the person apparently has a mental disorder of a nature or quality that will likely result in one or more of the following:

  - ○ serious bodily harm to the person

  - ○ serious bodily harm to another person

○   imminent and serious physical impairment

In order for Susan to see that her uncle received the help he needed, it was necessary for her to swear an oath (sometimes called an affidavit) and present it to a justice of the peace. Convinced of the serious nature of the situation, the justice issued a Form 2. The police accompanied the ambulance attendants to George's room where he was taken into custody. He was taken to the local hospital where he was assessed and treated for dehydration and pneumonia. Following his physical recovery he was assessed by a doctor (an evaluator) and found to be mentally capable of consenting to admission to a care facility. Based on his own consent, he was placed in a long term care facility.

The case of George Williams represents an exceptional situation, but the law provides for exceptions like this where extreme measures may be necessary. Hopefully, it is apparent that while the law in Ontario gives people certain decision making rights and protects those rights through an appeal process, it also provides for emergency situations where the life of an incapable person and/or those caring for them may be at great risk.

Emergency Treatment without Consent

An emergency is evident if the person is apparently experiencing severe suffering or is at risk, if treatment is not administered promptly, of sustaining serious bodily harm (*Health Care Consent Act* (section 25)).

There is provision for treatment to be administered without consent to an incapable person if, in the opinion of the health practitioner proposing the treatment, there is:

- an emergency

- delay in obtaining consent or refusal from a substitute decision maker would prolong the person's suffering and put the person at risk of sustaining serious bodily harm.

There is provision for treatment to be administered without consent to a capable person when:

- there is an emergency

- communication is not possible

- efforts have been made to overcome the communication barrier

- delay would prolong suffering or put the person at risk of bodily harm

- there is no reason to believe the person would not want the treatment

If treatment is administered in an emergency, it can only be continued for as long as is reasonably necessary to find:

- the incapable person's substitute decision maker and obtain consent or refusal, or

- a practical means of communicating with the capable person so that they can give or refuse consent.

Gunter Keller is a member of the Kingdom Hall of Jehovah's Witnesses. Based on the teachings of his church and his own beliefs, Gunter would not want to receive any blood or blood products in the event of a medical emergency. He carries a wallet size card with him that gives specific instructions regarding his beliefs and suggests treatment options that are acceptable to him. Last winter Gunter was rushed to the emergency department of the local hospital following a skiing accident. He was unconscious and had lost a lot of blood from a compound fracture of the femur. Gunter's wife, Irmgard, had been contacted and met the ambulance at the hospital. Irmgard is not Jehovah's Witness but is aware of Gunter's request. She found the instruction card in Gunter's wallet and as his attorney for personal care refused a blood transfusion on his behalf but gave consent for normal saline to be given intravenously.

Even in situations where there is an emergency, the health practitioner and the attorney are bound to follow any wishes that are known and are applicable to the situation, assuming that the person expressed relevant wishes while mentally capable. Section 26 of the *Health Care Consent Act* states that a health practitioner shall not administer an emergency treatment (section 25) if the health practitioner has reasonable grounds to believe that the person, while capable and after attaining 16 years of age, expressed a wish applicable to the circumstances to refuse consent to treatment.

As we end this chapter, **Important Things to Remember are:**

- The *Substitute Decisions Act* makes it possible for an attorney to use reasonable force that is necessary with respect to assessment or treatment of an incapable person when the Power of Attorney for Personal Care has this special provision written into it and the required assessment procedures have been followed.

- The verbal objection of an incapable person does not necessarily cancel the authority of an attorney for personal care or substitute decision maker to make a decision.

- The *Mental Health Act* makes provision for extreme situations where the life of an incapable person or their care giver may be at risk.

- The *Health Care Consent Act* makes provision for treatment to be administered without consent in emergency situations.

Conclusion

The development of laws for substitute decision making in Ontario was, to a great extent, prompted by a concern for vulnerable adults. Without laws to protect the management of property, some people were easy prey for those who would take advantage of them. Without laws to protect personal care decision making, many people suffered neglect and sometimes abuse. The laws we have now represent a great step forward, but the need to balance the decision making rights of individuals with society's obligation to protect its vulnerable members, sometimes leaves gaps.

For the average citizen, however, the present laws both protect and enhance decision making rights. Consideration of your need for powers of attorney is an important part of financial and estate planning. A power of attorney is a very powerful document and should always be prepared with as much foresight and understanding as possible. If you already have powers of attorney, they should be reviewed every two or three years, or sooner, if your situation warrants it. As your life situation and relationships change, it is more than likely that your powers of attorney will require change.

The laws governing powers of attorney are detailed and complex, but after reading this book I hope you have an understanding of the basics and feel that you can use the book as a reference in the future. Unlike your will which benefits your family after you've died, powers of attorney benefit you in the here and now. Here's hoping that you are willing and able to take advantage of this.

Appendix A

Determination of Mental Capacity and Substitute Decision Making

FIGURE 1

The *Substitute Decisions Act* is the law that governs the giving of a Power of Attorney for Personal Care and/or a Continuing Power of Attorney for Property.

Who determines if a person is mentally capable of giving a power of attorney?

Criteria indicating capacity to give a Continuing Power of Attorney for Property are listed in section 8 of the *Substitute Decisions Act*.

Criteria indicating capacity to give a Power of Attorney for Personal Care are listed in section 47(1) of the same Act.

Anyone assisting in the preparation of a power of attorney should be aware of these criteria and confident that the grantor is capable.

The law does not designate a specific person to determine the capacity of another person to give a power of attorney.

If a person is mentally incapable of giving a power of attorney can someone else do this for them?

If a person is mentally incapable of giving a power of attorney, no one else can do this on their behalf.

Note: A person may be incapable of managing property, but capable of giving a Continuing Power of Attorney for Property. Also, a person may be incapable of making personal care decisions, but capable of giving a Power of Attorney for Personal Care.

FIGURE 2

The Substitute Decisions Act is the law that governs property management for an incapable person.

Who determines if a person is mentally incapable of managing his or her property and finances?

Mental capacity can be determined according to instructions that the grantor writes in his or her Continuing Power of Attorney for Property. For example, the grantor may request that his or her lawyer or accountant determine his or her capacity to manage property before releasing the power of attorney document to the attorney.

If the Continuing Power of Attorney for Property states that it is only effective when the grantor becomes incapable, but the document doesn't say how incapacity is to be determined, then,

a) an assessor trained by the Attorney General can determine mental capacity to manage property; or

b) a physician working is accordance with the Mental Health Act can determine mental capacity to manage property. In this case the person would be an in-patient in a psychiatric facility.

If a person is mentally incapable of managing property or finances, who makes property and finance decisions for him or her?

A court-appointed guardian can make property decisions for an incapable person.

A statutory guardian can make property decisions for an incapable person.

An attorney operating under a Continuing Power of Attorney for Property can make property decisions for an incapable person.

FIGURE 3

The *Substitute Decisions Act* is the law governing personal care decisions for an incapable person. Note: This applies to personal care decisions that are not covered by the *Health Care Consent Act.*

Who determines if a person is mentally incapable of making non Health Care Consent Act personal care decisions?

The Substitute Decisions Act (section 49 (1)(b)) allows the attorney to determine whether the grantor is incapable of making personal care decisions if there is no provision in the power of attorney stating otherwise.

Capacity can be determined according to instructions that the grantor writes in his or her Power of Attorney for Personal Care; that is, the grantor may want a doctor to determine his or her mental capacity to make personal care decisions.

If the Power of Attorney for Personal Care states that it is only effective in the event of the grantor's incapacity and doesn't provide a method for determining this, then the attorney is only authorized to act when they receive notice from a capacity assessor confirming that the grantor has been assessed and is incapable of personal care.

If a person is mentally incapable of making these personal care decisions, who makes these decisions for him or her?

A court-appointed guardian of person can make personal care decisions for an incapable person.

An attorney operating under a Power of Attorney for Personal Care can make personal care decisions for an incapable person.

FIGURE 4

The *Health Care Consent Act* is the law that governs three types of health care decisions for an incapable person: decisions related to treatment, admission to a Long Term Care facility and personal assistance services in a Long Term Care facility.

Who determines if the person is mentally incapable of making health care decisions covered under the *Health Care Consent Act*?

For treatment:

A health care practitioner as defined in the *Health Care Consent Act* (section 2) must determine if a person is mentally capable of giving his or her consent to the proposed treatment.

For admission to a Long Term Care facility:

An evaluator as defined in the *Health Care Consent Act* (section 2) must determine if a person is mentally capable of consenting to admission to a care facility.

For personal assistance services in a Long Term Care facility:

An evaluator as defined in the *Health Care Consent Act* (section 2) must determine if the person is mentally capable of personal assistance services.

If the person is mentally incapable of making these health care decisions, who makes health care decisions for him or her?

Under the *Health Care Consent Act* the following persons can make health care decisions for an incapable person. These are listed in order of authority.

- court-appointed guardian of person

- attorney for personal care

- board appointed representative

- other substitute decision maker

  o spouse or partner

  o child or parent

  o parent with only right of access

  o sibling

  o any other relative

Appendix B

Decision Making Processes

FIGURE 1: Property Decisions under the *Substitute Decisions Act*

A court-appointed guardian of property is the highest ranking decision maker for a person who is incapable of managing his or her property. If there is no guardian of property, the next highest ranking decision maker is an attorney for property.

Is there an attorney for property?

→ Yes   Attorney acts in accordance with conditions and restrictions in the Continuing Power of Attorney for Property

→ No   Is the person capable of appointing an attorney for property?

    → Yes   Person may appoint an attorney for property to act on his or her behalf.

    → No   Evaluate other options:

       1. Application for formal assessment by a capacity assessor can be made by anyone if the person has not given power of attorney and is alleged to be incapable of managing his or her property.

Assessed as capable	→	Person continues to make their own decisions.
Assessed as incapable	→	Public Guardian and Trustee becomes the person's statutory guardian, but will transfer statutory guardianship to a family member who is approved by the Public Guardian and Trustee's office.

       2. Public Guardian and Trustee investigation of serious adverse effects

Evidence of serious adverse effects	→	Public Guardian and Trustee applies to the court for temporary guardianship.
No evidence of serious adverse effects	→	Continued support from family, friends, and community agencies.

FIGURE 1　Commentary	Reference in Law *Substitute Decisions Act*	Reference in *Willing and Able*
A person who is incapable of managing their property sometimes may be angry and/or resistant to the help of their attorney for property. This is difficult behaviour which needs to be managed. In this situation and if there are no conditions or restrictions, the attorney has the authority to act when they have possession of a valid Continuing Power of Attorney for Property.	sections 7(1), 9	pages 51-52, 70
A person may be incapable of managing their property but still capable of appointing an attorney for property.	section 9	pages 40, 48
Where there is no guardian of property or attorney for property the *Substitute Decisions Act* provides for the formal assessment of a person's mental capacity to manage property.	section 16	pages 56-59, 71
The Public Guardian and Trustee (PGT) becomes the person's statutory guardian of property if a capacity assessor issues a certificate of incapacity or if a certificate of incapacity is issued under the Mental Health Act. The PGT will transfer the statutory guardianship to a family member who is approved by the PGT's office.	sections 15, 16(1)	pages 67-69
A finding of incapacity that results in statutory guardianship can be appealed to the Consent and Capacity Board.	section 16(6)	pages 59, 62
Serious adverse effects include loss of a significant part of a person's property or failure to provide the necessities of life for him or herself, or their dependents.	section 27(1)	page 63
Investigation of serious adverse effects by the PGT does not always require a home visit.	section 27(3)	page 63
If the PGT finds evidence of serious adverse effects the PGT will apply to the court to be appointed the person's temporary guardian of property.	section 27(3.1)	page 63

FIGURE 2   Personal Care Decisions under the *Health Care Consent Act*

Type of Decision: Personal Care
- treatment
- admission to a care facility
- personal assistance services in a care facility

Capacity to give consent for these decisions is determined by:
- a health practitioner
- an evaluator

If the person is incapable, who gives consent?

Is there a Guardian
of the Person?   →   Yes   Guardian gives or withholds consent.

→   No   Is there an attorney for personal care?

→   Yes
Attorney gives or withholds consent according to the person's instructions while capable or best interests.

→   No
Is person capable of giving Power of Attorney for Personal Care?

→   Yes
Person may appoint an attorney who can act on his or her behalf.

→   No   Consent is given by:
- a Board appointed rep.
- spouse, partner
- parent, child
- brother, sister
- other relative

FIGURE 2 Commentary	Reference in Law *Health Care Consent Act*	Reference in *Willing and Able*
The *Health Care Consent Act* provides a process for making personal care decisions in three areas: treatment, admission to a care facility and personal assistance services in a care facility.	section 1	pages 28-29, 92-99
A health practitioner determines a person's mental capacity to make a treatment decision.	section 10	pages 92-93
An evaluator determines a person's mental capacity to give consent for admission to a care facility or for personal assistance services in a care facility.	sections 40, 57(1)	page 97
A finding of incapacity by a health practitioner or an evaluator can be appealed to the Consent and Capacity Board.	sections 32(1), 50(1), 65(1)	pages 94, 128
A guardian of person is the highest ranking decision maker and is appointed by the court.	section 20(1)	pages 95, 106
An attorney for personal care is the second highest ranking decision maker and is appointed by the grantor in a Power of Attorney for Personal Care.	section 20(1)	pages 85-87, 95, 107
A person may be incapable of making personal care decisions but still capable of appointing an attorney for personal care in a Power of Attorney for Personal Care.	section 47	page 41
If there is no guardian of person or attorney for personal care and the person is incapable of giving consent for him or herself, the *Substitute Decisions Act* provides a list of substitute decision makers.	section 20(1)	page 95

FIGURE 3 (a)   Personal Care Decisions under the *Substitute Decisions Act* (with an attorney for personal care)

Type of Decision: Personal Care decisions that do not come under the *Health Care Consent Act* include health care, nutrition, clothing, shelter, safety, and hygiene.

Examples: bathing at home (hygiene)
admission to a private retirement home (shelter)

Is there an attorney for personal care?

→   Yes   An attorney for personal care can only act on the grantor's behalf when the grantor becomes mentally incapable of making the personal care decision.

1. If attorney's authority to act is contingent on a finding of mental incapacity and the power of attorney:

    a. includes a method
    The attorney may act when the method results in a finding of incapacity.

    b. does not include a method
    Formal assessment by a capacity assessor is required before the attorney can act.

2. If the attorney's authority is not contingent on a finding of incapacity, the attorney can determine whether the person is capable of making personal care decisions that come under the *Substitute Decisions Act*.

    If the grantor disagrees with the decision made by his or her attorney for personal care and if the grantor is capable of giving Power of Attorney for Personal Care, the grantor is also capable of revoking the Power of Attorney for Personal Care

    Note: For these types of decisions there is no provision in the law for the grantor to appeal a finding of incapacity to the Consent and Capacity Board.

FIGURE 3 (a)　　　　Commentary	Reference in Law *Substitute Decisions Act*	Reference In *Willing and Able*
The *Substitute Decisions Act* defines personal care as health care, nutrition, clothing, shelter, safety, and hygiene.	section 43	pages 18, 102
An attorney for personal care can only act on the grantor's behalf when the grantor is incapable of making a personal care decision.	section 49(1), 66(3)	page 102
If the grantor requires a finding of incapacity before the attorney can act, the grantor may include a method in the Power of Attorney for Personal Care by which his or her capacity for personal care is to be determined.	section 49(1)(b)	pages 103, 107
If the Power of Attorney for Personal Care requires a finding of incapacity before the attorney can act and does not provide a method, a formal assessment by a capacity assessor is required before the attorney can act.	section 49(2)	pages 103, 107
If there are no conditions or restrictions, the attorney for personal care can determine whether the grantor is capable of making a personal care decision.	section 49(1)(b)	pages 103, 105, 108, 112
There is no appeal to the Consent and Capacity Board for personal care decisions that come under the *Substitute Decisions Act*.	no provision	page 128
If a grantor is capable of giving power of attorney, he or she is capable of revoking the power of attorney.	section 47	page 103

FIGURE 3 (b)   Personal Care Decisions under the *Substitute Decisions Act* (when there is no attorney for personal care)

Type of Decision: Personal Care decisions that do not come under the *Health Care Consent Act* include health care, nutrition, clothing, shelter, safety, and hygiene.

Examples: bathing at home (hygiene)
admission to a private retirement home (shelter)

Is there an attorney for personal care?

→   No

Is the person capable of appointing an attorney for personal care?

→   Yes   Appoint an attorney for personal care

→   No   Evaluate other options:

1.   Continued support from family and community.

2.   Public Guardian and Trustee investigation of serious adverse effects

Note: The Public Guardian and Trustee has an obligation to investigate serious adverse effects. The Public Guardian and Trustee is not obligated to go out or to take any steps that in their opinion are unnecessary. For example, if family and agencies are involved, they may choose to leave follow up with them.

Evidence of serious adverse effects
→   Public Guardian and Trustee may apply to the court for temporary guardianship

Note: Very often it is the investigation of serious adverse effects related to property that results in temporary guardianship and subsequently personal care needs are also addressed.

3.   Does the *Mental Health Act* apply?
→   Form 1
→   Form 2

FIGURE 3 (b)　　　Commentary	Reference in Law *Substitute Decisions Act*	Reference in *Willing and Able*
The *Substitute Decisions Act* defines personal care as health care, nutrition, clothing, shelter, safety, and hygiene.	section 43	pages 18, 102
A person is capable of appointing an attorney for personal care if he or she understands that the proposed attorney has a genuine concern for his or her welfare and that the proposed attorney may have to make personal care decisions on his or her behalf.	section 47(1)	page 41
Serious adverse effects of the person include serious illness or injury, or deprivation of liberty or personal security.	section 62(1)	page 107
The Public Guardian and Trustee has a duty to investigate any allegation that a person is incapable of personal care and that serious adverse effects are occurring or may occur as a result.	section 62(2)	page 107
The Public Guardian and Trustee is not obligated to take any steps, that in his or her opinion, are unnecessary for the purpose of determining whether an application for temporary guardianship is required.	section 62(3)	page 107
Provisions of the *Mental Health Act* may apply.	*Mental Health Act*, sections 15, 16	pages 135, 136

Appendix C
Glossary

Assessor   An assessor is a person who conducts assessments of mental capacity under the *Substitute Decisions Act.* The assessor's role and responsibilities are described in the *Substitute Decisions Act.* Assessors do not play any role under the *Health Care Consent Act.*

Attorney   An attorney is the person(s) whom you appoint in a power of attorney to represent you and act on your behalf. An attorney may also be referred to as a grantee or donee.

Capacity   The concept of capacity, as used in the *Substitute Decisions Act* and *Health Care Consent Act*, is the ability to understand and appreciate information relevant to making a decision and the ability to understand the reasonably, foreseeable consequences of a decision or lack of decision.

Care facility

Care facilities, mentioned in the *Health Care Consent Act,* refer to nursing homes and homes for the aged. These long term care institutions receive funding from the Ministry of Health to cover the cost of programs and services. Residents of these facilities pay a government established rate to cover the cost of their room and board.

Consent and Capacity Board

The Consent and Capacity Board is an independent tribunal that hears cases under the *Mental Health Act*, the *Substitute Decisions Act*, the *Health Care Consent Act*, and the *Long Term Care Act.* The *Health Care Consent Act* contains the legislative authority under which the Consent and Capacity Board operates.

Continuing   This is a term used to describe a power of attorney for property that can be effective before incapacity and continues to be effective after incapacity.

Evaluator   Under the *Health Care Consent Act*, an evaluator is a person who is able to assess capacity to make a decision about admission to a care facility or a personal assistance service (*Health Care Consent Act,* section 1).

Fiduciary   A fiduciary is a person in a position of trust. A fiduciary must always act in the best interests of the person for whom the fiduciary is acting and must avoid any conflict between his or her own interests and the interests of the person for whom the fiduciary is acting.

Guardian of the Person

A guardian of the person is a person designated by a court order under the *Substitute Decisions Act* to make personal care decisions for an incapable person.

Guardian of Property

A guardian of property is a person designated by a court order under the *Substitute Decisions Act* to make property decisions for an incapable person.

Health Practitioner

For purposes of the *Health Care Consent Act*, members of the following professional groups are health practitioners:

Audiologists	Physicians
Chiropodists	Physiotherapists
Chiropractors	Podiatrists
Dentists	Nurses
Dental Hygienists	Registered Social Workers and
Dietitians	Social Service Workers
Denturists	Respiratory Therapists
Midwives	Medical Radiation Technologists
Massage Therapists	Medical Laboratory Technologists
Occupational Therapists	Speech-Language Pathologists
Optometrists	

Naturopaths under the *Drugless Practitioners Act*

Office of the Public Guardian and Trustee

The Public Guardian and Trustee (PGT) operates under the authority of the Ministry of the Attorney General. The PGT has various responsibilities related to the protection of incapable people and their property and acts as a last resort decision maker regarding treatment and admission to long term care facilities.

Ontario Superior Court of Justice

Ontario's senior trial court which hears appeals from the Consent and Capacity Board and applications for guardianship under the *Substitute Decisions Act*.

Partner   Any two people who have resided together for one year or more and have a meaningful relationship. The definition is broad and allows for multiple relationships, including same sex relationships.

Personal Assistance Service

Term used in the *Health Care Consent Act* to describe activities of daily living in a care facility such as ambulation, dressing, eating and washing in a care facility.

Personal Care

Under the *Substitute Decisions Act*, personal care includes health care, nutrition, clothing, shelter, hygiene, and safety.

Power of Attorney for Personal Care

A legally recognized document by which an individual gives someone else the authority to make personal care decisions on his or her behalf in the event of incapacity. A Power of Attorney for Personal Care must be made in accordance with procedures set out in the *Substitute Decisions Act*.

Continuing Power of Attorney for Property

A legally recognized document by which an individual gives someone else the authority to make property decisions on his or her behalf while mentally capable and/or in the event of incapacity. A Continuing Power of Attorney for Property must be made in accordance with procedures set out in the *Substitute Decisions Act*.

Property   Property refers to bank accounts, investments, business holdings, chattels such as furniture or cars, real estate, and intellectual property such as copyrights, patents or trade marks.

Property Management

Property management refers to financial decisions/transactions made in the course of managing income, assets and/or debt.

Representative

A representative is a person appointed by the Consent and Capacity Board to make decisions about treatment, admission to a care facility, or personal assistance services on behalf of an incapable person.

Revocation   Revocation means to cancel or to void.

Statutory Guardian

A statutory guardian is a person who has been given the legal authority to manage someone else's property because the person has been assessed and found to be incapable of managing his or her own property. The finding of incapacity may be made by a physician under the *Mental Health Act* or an assessor under the *Substitute Decisions Act*. Immediately upon a finding of incapacity the Public Guardian and Trustee becomes the statutory guardian. If there is a family member to assume this role, they may apply to replace the Public Guardian and Trustee as the incapable person's statutory guardian.

Serious Adverse Effects (personal care)

Serious illness or injury, or deprivation of liberty or personal security are defined as serious adverse effects under the *Substitute Decisions Act*.

Serious Adverse Effects (property)

Failure to provide the necessities of life for him or herself or dependents, or loss of a significant part of a person's property are defined as serious adverse effects under the *Substitute Decisions Act*.

Spouse   Under the *Substitute Decisions Act* and the *Health Care Consent Act,* a spouse is a person of the opposite sex to whom the person is married or living in a conjugal relationship.

Substitute Decision Maker

A person who is authorized to make decisions on behalf of an incapable person, such as a guardian, an attorney, a Board appointed representative, a spouse, or a relative.

Treatment   Under the *Health Care Consent Act*, treatment includes anything that is done for a therapeutic, preventive, palliative, diagnostic, cosmetic or other health related purpose and includes a course or plan of treatment.

Index

Endnotes

1. *Substitute Decisions Act*, 1992, S.O. 1992, c.30

2. *Canadian Charter of Rights and Freedoms (Charter),* Part I of the *Constitution Act, 1982,* being Schedule B to the *Canada Act 1982* (U.K.), 1982, c. 11.

3. L.E. Rozovsky, *The Canadian Patient's Book of Rights* (Toronto: Doubleday Canada Ltd., 1980).

4. Ibid., pg.1

5. *Powers of Attorney Act*, R.S.O. 1990, c. P.20 (Amended 1992, c.32, s.24; proclaimed in force April 3, 1995)

6. *Health Care Consent Act, 1996*, S.O. 1996, c.2

7. *Advocacy Act, 1992*, S.O. 1992, c.26

8. *Consent to Treatment Act, 1992*, S.O. 1992, c.31

9. *Tenant Protection Act, 1997*, S.O. 1997, c.24

10. Michael Silberfeld and Arthur Fish, *When the Mind Fails*, (Toronto: University of Toronto Press Incorporated, 1994)